ADDITIONAL INCOME STREAMS

OPPORTUNITIES TO INVESTIGATE

CONNECTNOMADS   contact@connectnomads.com

CONTENTS

CONNECT NOMADS DIGITAL ELIBRARY

What is ConnectNomads.com

ConnectNomads.com is a comprehensive platform designed for digital nomads and remote workers seeking resources, guidance, and community. Offering valuable information on topics such as remote work opportunities, travel planning, and lifestyle management, ConnectNomads.com aims to empower location-independent professionals to thrive in their careers while exploring the world.

How this book is structured

This book is designed to serve as a comprehensive guide for digital nomads, offering insights and advice on various aspects of self-discovery and personal growth. It is not intended to be read in one go, but rather as a set of guidelines that provide valuable takeaways for different ideas and aspects of the nomadic lifestyle. As you explore the chapters, you may notice some overlap between topics, as certain strategies are commonly applicable across different areas of personal development. Feel free to read at your own pace, revisiting sections as needed, and drawing inspiration from the diverse range of concepts and techniques presented throughout the book.

If you have any ideas on new input, or even corrections, we are more than happy to hear from you, and if our editors like and accept the input then – if you are comfortable with it – we will include in our next update with credit noted for you.

Email us – contact@connectnomads.com

Mentions

We would like to clarify that throughout this book, we have not received any monetary gain or inducements for mentioning any connections, people, or resources. Our primary goal is to share valuable insights and tips that can genuinely help digital nomads in their journey of self-discovery and personal growth. The only exceptions to this are individuals or resources identified as ConnectNomads Members on our website. These members are part of our community and support our mission. We maintain transparency and prioritize the authenticity of the information shared, ensuring that our readers can trust the guidance provided in this book.

Our Digital Library

The ConnectNomads.com library offers members a diverse collection of free eBooks, providing invaluable insights and practical advice on a variety of topics related to the digital nomad lifestyle. From remote work strategies to travel tips and personal development, these eBooks are a valuable resource for location-independent professionals seeking to enhance their skills, knowledge, and overall experience.

Please visit http://www.connectnomad.com to see if there are any other publications which might interest you.

INTRODUCTION

Get Started

Are you ready to embrace a career that allows you to live your passion, achieve a healthy work-life balance, and earn a sustainable income? This guide presents the top self-employed job opportunities for everyone, from students to stay-at-home parents and 9-5 workers seeking a change. With self-employment on the rise, there has never been a better time to consider these opportunities.

In today's fast-paced, ever-evolving digital world, aspiring digital nomads must be prepared for the unexpected and ready to adapt to new challenges. A comprehensive how-to book that emphasizes the importance of diversifying income streams can serve as a valuable resource for those seeking a sustainable digital nomad lifestyle.

DIVERSIFY, DIVERSIFY, DIVERSIFY

Diversifying your income streams as a digital nomad offers numerous benefits, such as:

- **Financial Stability**: Relying on a sole source of income can be risky, especially when working remotely and dealing with clients from different industries and time zones. By diversifying income streams, digital nomads can mitigate the risks associated with income fluctuations, client attrition, and market changes, ensuring greater financial stability.

- **Flexibility and Adaptability**: Diverse income sources allow digital nomads to be more agile and responsive to changing market conditions, client needs, and personal circumstances. This flexibility can make it easier to pivot between different projects, industries, or even career paths as needed, without experiencing significant financial disruption.

- **Skill Development and Growth**: Pursuing multiple income streams often requires digital nomads to develop a broad range of skills and expertise. This continuous learning process can lead to personal and professional growth, making digital nomads more competitive in the global job market.

- **Creative Fulfilment**: Diversifying income streams can provide opportunities for digital nomads to explore different passions and interests, leading to a more fulfilling work-life balance. By engaging in diverse projects and roles, digital nomads can nurture their creativity and find new ways to grow both personally and professionally.

- **Building a Resilient Financial Future**: A diversified income portfolio can help digital nomads build a more resilient financial future. By leveraging multiple income sources, they can better prepare for unexpected challenges, such as economic downturns, health issues, or changes in personal circumstances.

First, we will start with the general skills required for every Digital Nomad job, anywhere.

General Skills
These Tips and Ideas are the more general which straddle all the Income Streams we have so far written about.

That said there is considerable similarities between some Streams, we have kept these in there with some additional guides specific to that idea.

Managing your finances as a Digital Nomad,

Managing your finances is essential to ensuring your long-term success and stability. This guide will provide you with essential tips and strategies for managing your finances effectively as a freelance writer.

1. Track your income and expenses:
    - Maintain a detailed record of your income and expenses to help you understand your financial situation, identify trends, and make informed decisions.
    - Use budgeting and expense tracking tools, such as Mint, YNAB, Freshbooks, Wave or QuickBooks, to streamline this process.
    - Staying organized will help you monitor your financial health and streamline the tax filing process.
    - Create a monthly budget that accounts for your living expenses, business costs, and savings goals.
    - Regularly review your budget and adjust as needed to ensure you are living within your means and achieving your financial objectives.

2. Open separate bank accounts:
    - Separate your personal and business finances by opening dedicated bank accounts for each. This can help you manage your money more effectively, simplify tax preparation, and maintain a clear distinction between your personal and professional expenses.

3. Set Aside Money for Taxes
    - As a self-employed professional, you are responsible for paying your own taxes. Estimate your tax liability for the year and set aside a portion of your earnings each month to cover your tax obligations. Open a separate savings account specifically for this purpose to avoid spending the funds unintentionally.

4. Understand Tax Regulations for Digital Nomads
    - Tax regulations for digital nomads vary based on your country of residence, income sources, and the countries you visit. Consult a tax professional or use online to help you understand and comply with the tax laws applicable to your situation.

5. Build an emergency fund:
    - Establish an emergency fund to cover unexpected expenses or income fluctuations. Aim to save at least three to six months' worth of living expenses to provide a financial safety net in case of emergencies.

6. Plan for retirement:

- Even as a digital nomad, planning for retirement is essential. Research retirement savings options, such as individual retirement accounts and contribute regularly to ensure you are financially prepared for the future.

7. Invest in your business:
   - Allocate a portion of your budget to investing in your freelance writing business, such as purchasing new equipment, attending workshops, or marketing your services. Investing in your business can help you grow and increase your earning potential.

8. Manage your cash flow:
   - Monitor your cash flow to ensure you have enough funds to cover your expenses and meet your financial obligations. Develop strategies for managing cash flow fluctuations, such as diversifying your income sources or negotiating payment terms with clients.

9. Set financial goals:
   - Establish short-term and long-term financial goals for your freelance writing business, such as increasing your income, paying off debt, or saving for a major purchase.
   - Regularly review your progress and adjust your strategies as needed to achieve your goals.
10. Consult a financial professional:
    - Consider working with a financial advisor or accountant who specializes in freelancing or small business finances. A professional can provide guidance on tax planning, retirement savings, and other financial matters to help you make informed decisions.

Organize travel arrangements and documentation

It is crucial to be well-prepared and organized when it comes to travel arrangements and documentation. This guide will provide tips on how to plan and organize your travel effectively, ensuring a smooth transition to your new assignment.

1. Plan your travel itinerary:
   - Once you have secured a house or pet sitting assignment, start planning your travel itinerary. Determine the most efficient and cost-effective route to reach your destination, considering factors such as distance, time, and budget.
   - Research transportation options, such as flights, trains, buses, or car rentals, and book your tickets in advance to secure the best deals.

2. Obtain necessary travel documents:
   - Ensure that you have a valid passport, visas, or any other required documentation for your destination.
   - Research the entry requirements for your destination country and apply for visas or permits well in advance to avoid last-minute complications. Also, make sure to keep digital and physical copies of your travel documents in case of loss or damage.

3. Plan Your Travel Arrangements
   - Carefully plan your travel arrangements, including flights, accommodations, and transportation. Use travel booking sites like Skyscanner, Airbnb, and Booking.com to find the best deals on airfare and lodging. Consider joining a co-living community or staying at a long-term rental to reduce accommodation costs and meet like-minded individuals.

4. Maintain a Valid Passport and Visas
   - Ensure your passport is up-to-date and has at least six months of validity remaining. Research visa requirements for the countries you plan to visit and apply for the necessary visas well in advance. Keep digital and physical copies of your travel documents in case of loss or theft.

5. Stay Informed About Vaccinations and Health Recommendations
   - Research the recommended vaccinations and health precautions for your travel destinations. Schedule appointments with your healthcare provider or a travel clinic to receive any necessary vaccinations before your departure. Additionally, stay informed about COVID-19 regulations and testing requirements, as these may impact your travel plans.

6. Purchase Travel Insurance
   - Invest in a comprehensive travel insurance policy that covers medical expenses, trip cancellations, and lost or stolen belongings. Companies like World Nomads, SafetyWing, and InsureMyTrip offer policies designed for digital nomads and long-term travellers.

7. Purchase travel insurance:
   - Invest in comprehensive travel insurance that covers medical expenses, trip cancellations, lost luggage, and other potential issues.
   - This will provide you with peace of mind and financial protection in the event of unforeseen circumstances during your travels.

8. Research local transportation options:
   - Familiarize yourself with local transportation options at your destination, such as public transport, taxis, or rideshare services. This will help you navigate your new surroundings more efficiently upon arrival.

9. Arrange for accommodations before and after your assignment:
   - If you need accommodations before your house or pet sitting assignment begins or after it ends, research and book suitable lodging in advance. This will ensure that you have a comfortable place to stay while you transition between assignments.

10. Coordinate your arrival with the anyone you are connecting with:
   - Communicate with all connections to coordinate your arrival time and any necessary details, such as where to pick up keys or how to access any property. This will help to ensure a smooth handover and avoid any miscommunication or delays.

11. Prepare a travel essentials kit:
   - Pack a travel essentials kit that includes items such as toiletries, medications, chargers, adapters, and any other items you may need during your travels. Having these items readily available will make your journey more comfortable and help you settle into your new assignment more quickly.

12. Create a digital itinerary and backup:
   - Organize your travel plans, including transportation, accommodations, and important contact information, in a digital itinerary. This can be stored on your smartphone or in a cloud-based service for easy access during your travels. Additionally, create a backup of your itinerary and travel documents in case your primary digital storage fails.

13. Inform your bank and credit card companies of your travel plans:
   - Notify your bank and credit card companies of your travel plans to avoid any potential issues with your accounts while abroad. This will help prevent any unexpected account freezes or declines due to suspected fraudulent activity.

14. Stay updated on travel advisories and local news:
   - Regularly check for travel advisories and local news updates for your destination to stay informed about any potential risks, changes in regulations, or other valuable information that may impact your travels or assignment.

BLOGGING

Starting a blog can be an excellent way to make extra money and create a lifestyle business. While it requires some initial effort, blogging can eventually generate enough income to replace your traditional job. In this comprehensive guide, we will walk you through the process of starting a successful blog, from choosing a niche to monetizing your content.

Have you ever wondered how successful digital nomads make a living by running a blog and traveling the world? It is a result of hard work, dedication, and following the principles outlined in this guide.

With over 600 million blogs in 2023, the competition is fierce. To stand out and embrace the digital nomad lifestyle, you need more than just a website and internet connection. This guide will walk you through the process of monetizing your blog, so you can finally leave that 9-to-5 behind. How much can bloggers earn?

Blogging can be a lucrative venture if done correctly. Some bloggers make anywhere from $500 to $2,000 per month in their first year, and up to $30,000 per month with a large audience. Your income will depend on factors like your niche and monetization strategies.

When can you start earning money from your blog?

The timeline for monetizing your blog depends on factors such as your niche, the effort you put in, and your monetization strategies. Some people take a few months, while others need a few years to build a steady following. Be patient and consistently create valuable content.

Top seven ways to make money from your blog.

1. Sell your services:
   - Offer freelance services related to your blog's niche, such as authoring articles, designing logos, or programming websites.

2. Turn your blogs into an eBook:
   - Compile your best blog posts into an eBook and sell it on platforms like Amazon.

3. Sell a physical or digital product:
   - Create a product line relevant to your readers and find a manufacturer to produce them on-demand.
   - Alternatively, sell digital products like eBooks, online courses, or printable worksheets.

4. Write reviews for sponsored products:
   - Partner with brands to write sponsored reviews of their products, but make sure to disclose the sponsorship and be honest in your review.

5. Sell advertising:

- Partner with companies or use advertising networks like Google AdSense or AdThrive to sell ad space on your blog.

6. Affiliate marketing:
   - Promote products relevant to your audience and earn a commission from each sale through affiliate marketing programs.

7. Coaching or consulting:
   - Offer your expertise as a coach or consultant to help others succeed in the blogging world.

Key elements to make your blog profitable

1. A profitable niche:
   - Choose a niche that you are knowledgeable about, has low competition, and offers monetization potential.

2. A robust email list:
   - Build an email list to maintain relationships with your readers and promote products or services they might be interested in.

3. Learn about SEO:
   - Optimize your content for search engines by researching keywords, ranking in search engines, and building a solid SEO strategy.

With the right approach and dedication, you can successfully monetize your blog and live the digital nomad lifestyle of which you have always dreamt.

Choosing the Perfect Niche for Your Blog

Finding a unique and profitable niche for your blog can make all the difference in your success. This guide is designed to help you navigate the process of selecting a niche that is both interesting and lucrative, allowing you to share your experiences and generate income as you travel the world.

1. Identify your passions and interests:
   - Begin by listing your passions, hobbies, and areas of expertise. This will help you narrow down potential topics and ensure you will be able to produce content that is both engaging and authentic. Your enthusiasm for the subject matter will shine through, making it more likely that readers will connect with your content and keep coming back for more.

2. Research the competition:
   - Investigate other blogs and websites within your potential niches. This will give you a sense of the level of competition and help you determine if there's room for your unique perspective.
   - Look for gaps in the market or topics that have not been thoroughly covered. By identifying these opportunities, you can set your blog apart from the rest.

3. Determine profitability:

- Consider potential revenue streams for each niche, such as affiliate marketing, sponsored content, or digital products. Some niches may offer higher earning potential than others, so you will need to weigh the importance of pursuing your passion versus generating income. Research trending keywords and phrases within each niche to better understand what readers are searching for and the potential for monetization.

4. Assess your target audience:
   - Define the target audience for each niche by considering factors such as age, location, and interests. This will help you create content that resonates with your readers and increases engagement.
   - Additionally, understanding your audience will allow you to better tailor marketing strategies and promotional efforts.

5. Evaluate long-term potential:
   - Choose a niche that has the potential for long-term growth and sustainability. Trends and popular topics can change quickly, so it is important to select a subject matter that will remain relevant and interesting to your audience over time.
   - Consider the future of your niche and whether it has the potential to evolve alongside your own interests and experiences.

6. Test the waters:
   - Before fully committing to a niche, consider creating some sample content to gauge audience interest and engagement.
   - Share these posts on social media or within relevant online communities to gather feedback and analyse response. This will help you determine if the niche you have chosen is viable and worth investing time and effort into.

Selecting the Ideal Blogging Platform

Selecting the right blogging platform is crucial for creating a successful online presence. In this guide, we will walk you through the process of choosing a platform that meets your needs, accommodates your unique lifestyle, and helps you share your journey with the world.

1. Define your needs and goals:
   - Before selecting a platform, consider your blogging goals and requirements.
   - Are you looking to create a personal travel diary or build a professional brand?
   - Do you plan to monetize your blog, or is it primarily a creative outlet?
   - Identifying your objectives will help you choose a platform that aligns with your vision.

2. Consider your technical expertise:
   - Blogging platforms vary in their complexity and ease of use. If you are a beginner or prefer a user-friendly interface, opt for a platform with an intuitive design and built-in features.
   - For those with more technical experience, consider a platform that offers greater customization and control over your blog's appearance and functionality.

3. Assess available features and customization:
   - Compare the features offered by different platforms to ensure they meet your needs.
   - Look for options such as social media integration, analytics tools, and search engine optimization (SEO) capabilities.

- Additionally, consider the extent to which each platform allows customization, as this will impact your blog's design and overall aesthetic.
- Evaluate costs and pricing plans: Blogging platforms often offer a range of pricing plans with varying features and capabilities. Determine your budget and compare the costs of each platform, considering potential expenses like domain registration, hosting fees, and premium themes or plugins. Be mindful of any limitations associated with free plans, as these may impact your ability to grow and monetize your blog.

4. Explore available support and resources:
   - As a digital nomad, you will need a blogging platform with reliable support and access to resources, as you may encounter technical issues or require assistance while on the road.
   - Research the customer support options available for each platform, such as live chat, email, or community forums.
   - Additionally, consider the availability of tutorials, documentation, and other educational resources.

5. Review platform reputation and community:
   - Investigate the reputation and user community surrounding each blogging platform.
   - Look for testimonials, reviews, and case studies from other digital nomads or bloggers within your niche. A strong community can provide invaluable support, inspiration, and networking opportunities as you grow your blog.

6. Test the platform:
   - Before committing to a platform, sign up for a free trial or create a test account to explore its features and usability. This hands-on experience will give you a better understanding of how the platform works and help you make an informed decision.

Purchasing a Domain Name and Web Hosting for Your Blog

Establishing a strong online presence starts with purchasing a domain name and web hosting for your blog. This guide will walk you through the process of selecting and acquiring a domain name and hosting plan that suits your needs and sets the foundation for your blogging success.

1. Choose a memorable domain name:
   - Your domain name is your blog's unique address on the internet, so it is essential to select a name that is memorable, relevant, and easy to spell.
   - Consider incorporating keywords related to your niche or opt for a creative and catchy name that reflects your personality and brand.
   - Stick to popular top-level domains (TLDs) like .com, .net, or .org for better recognition and search engine performance.

2. Research domain registrars:
   - Domain registrars are companies that manage the registration of domain names.
   - Research reputable registrars and compare their pricing, features, and customer support. Look for registrars that offer domain privacy protection, as this shields your personal information from being publicly visible in WHOIS records.

3. Check domain availability:
   - Use the domain search tools provided by registrars to check the availability of your desired domain name.

- If your chosen name is taken, consider alternative TLDs or slight variations in spelling or phrasing.

4. Determine your hosting needs:
   - Web hosting refers to the storage space and resources provided by a hosting company to make your blog accessible on the internet.
   - Evaluate your hosting needs based on factors such as expected traffic, storage requirements, and the complexity of your website.
   - For new bloggers, shared hosting is typically sufficient, while more established sites may require VPS, cloud, or dedicated hosting for better performance and resources.

5. Compare web hosting providers:
   - Research reputable web hosting providers and compare their plans, pricing, features, and customer support.
   - Look for providers that offer reliable uptime, fast loading speeds, and easy scalability as your blog grows.
   - Additionally, consider the availability of one-click installations for popular content management systems (CMS) like WordPress, as this simplifies the setup process.

6. Bundle domain and hosting:
   - Many domain registrars and web hosting providers offer bundled packages that include both domain registration and hosting services. Opting for a bundle can save you money and streamline the setup process.
   - However, be sure to weigh the pros and cons of bundling versus keeping these services separate, as it may be more difficult to switch providers in the future if you are unhappy with their performance.

7. Complete the purchase:
   - Once you have selected a domain name and hosting plan, follow the provider's checkout process to complete your purchase.
   - Be prepared to provide personal information for domain registration and payment details for both the domain and hosting services.
   - Keep track of your account credentials and any relevant documentation for future reference.

Designing Your Blog for Success and Engagement

The design of your blog plays a crucial role in attracting and retaining readers. A well-designed blog not only showcases your content but also reflects your unique personality and brand. This guide will help you create an engaging and visually appealing blog that resonates with your audience and supports your blogging goals.

1. Choose a Content Management System (CMS):
   - Selecting a user-friendly CMS is the first step in designing your blog.
   - Platforms like WordPress, Wix, and Squarespace offer intuitive interfaces, pre-built themes, and customizable features that make it easy to create and manage your blog.
   - Consider factors such as ease of use, available features, and community support when selecting a CMS.

2. Select a responsive theme or template:

- Choose a theme or template that aligns with your blog's niche and aesthetic preferences.
- Opt for a responsive design that automatically adapts to various screen sizes and devices, ensuring a seamless browsing experience for all readers.
- Keep in mind that premium themes may offer more features and customization options than free alternatives.

3. Customise your theme:
   - Once you have selected a theme, customize it to reflect your brand and personality.
   - Experiment with colour schemes, typography, and layout options to create a cohesive and visually appealing design.
   - Remember that simplicity and consistency are key; avoid clutter and ensure your design choices enhance your content rather than distract from it.

4. Create a compelling homepage:
   - Your homepage is often the first impression visitors have of your blog, so it is essential to make it visually appealing and easy to navigate. Include a clear and engaging header, an eye-catching hero image, and a concise introduction to your blog and its purpose.
   - Organize your content in a way that is easy to browse and highlights your most popular or recent posts.

5. Develop a clear navigation structure:
   - Ensure your blog is easy to navigate by creating a clear and intuitive menu structure. Include essential pages such as your "About" page, a "Contact" page, and any relevant categories or tags.
   - Ensure your menu is accessible from all pages and consider including a search bar for added convenience.

6. Optimise for readability:
   - Make your content easy to read by selecting a legible font, using proper formatting, and breaking up large blocks of text with headings, bullet points, or images.
   - Ensure there's sufficient contrast between your text and background colours and avoid using overly stylized or small fonts that may be difficult to read.

7. Incorporate multimedia elements:
   - Enhance your blog posts with relevant images, videos, and other multimedia elements. Visual content not only adds interest and variety but also helps break up text and improve readability.
   - Be sure to use high-quality images, optimize file sizes for fast loading, and properly credit any borrowed content.

8. Encourage social sharing and engagement:
   - Make it easy for readers to share your content on social media by incorporating share buttons on your blog posts.
   - Additionally, enable comments and engage with your audience by responding to their questions and feedback. This fosters a sense of community and encourages readers to return to your blog for future updates.

Creating Quality Content for Your Blog

Creating quality content is essential for building an engaged audience, establishing your authority within your niche, and driving traffic to your blog. This guide will provide you with tips and strategies to craft compelling, informative, and engaging content that resonates with your readers and supports your blogging goals.

1. Know your audience:
   - Understand the demographics, interests, and preferences of your target audience.
   - This will help you create content that speaks to their needs, desires, and pain points.
   - Tailor your writing style, tone, and topics to match your audience's preferences, ensuring your content is both relatable and valuable.

2. Focus on your niche:
   - Stay focused on your chosen niche and share your unique perspective and experiences as a digital nomad.
   - By consistently providing content related to your niche, you will establish yourself as an authority within the field and attract readers who are genuinely interested in your subject matter.

3. Prioritise storytelling:
   - Incorporate storytelling elements into your content to create a captivating narrative that draws readers in and keeps them engaged.
   - Share personal anecdotes, challenges, and triumphs to humanize your content and make it more relatable.
   - Be genuine and authentic in your storytelling to forge a deeper connection with your audience.

4. Provide valuable information:
   - Ensure your content offers value to your readers by providing useful tips, insights, and resources.
   - Focus on solving problems, answering questions, or addressing common concerns within your niche.
   - Conduct thorough research and provide accurate, up-to-date information to maintain credibility and trust with your audience.

5. Use a compelling headline:
   - Craft a captivating headline that piques your readers' curiosity and encourages them to click through to your content.
   - Use strong, actionable language, and include keywords related to your topic.
   - Keep your headline clear and concise, ensuring it accurately reflects the content of your post.

6. Optimize for readability:
   - Break up large blocks of text with headings, subheadings, bullet points, and images to make your content more visually appealing and easier to read.
   - Use short paragraphs, conversational language, and avoid jargon or overly complex terminology.
   - Properly format your content to guide readers through your post and make it more digestible.

7. Edit and proofread:
   - Thoroughly edit and proofread your content to ensure it is free from grammatical errors, spelling mistakes, and awkward phrasing.

- Ask a friend or use editing tools like Grammarly to help identify any errors you may have missed.
- Well-polished content not only appears more professional but also enhances your credibility as a writer.

8. Incorporate multimedia elements:
   - Enhance your content with relevant images, videos, infographics, or other multimedia elements.
   - Visual content can help illustrate your points, break up text, and improve reader engagement.
   - Always use high-quality visuals and optimize file sizes for faster loading times.

9. Engage with your audience:
   - Encourage readers to share their thoughts, experiences, and questions in the comments section of your blog posts.
   - Respond to comments and engage in conversations to foster a sense of community and show your readers that you value their input and feedback.

Optimising Your Content for SEO to Boost Visibility and Traffic

Optimising your blog content for search engine optimization (SEO) is essential for driving organic traffic, increasing visibility, and reaching a wider audience. This guide will provide you with essential tips and strategies for optimizing your content to rank higher on search engines and attract more readers to your blog.

1. Conduct keyword research:
   - Identify the most relevant and popular keywords within your niche by using keyword research tools like Google Keyword Planner, Ahrefs, or SEMrush. These tools help you uncover search terms with high search volume and low competition, which can improve your chances of ranking higher in search results.

2. Optimize your title and headings:
   - Incorporate your target keyword in the title of your blog post, as well as in the headings and subheadings throughout your content. This signals to search engines that your content is relevant to the keyword and helps improve your chances of ranking higher for that term.

3. Use your keywords naturally:
   - Integrate your target keywords throughout your content in a natural and organic manner. Avoid keyword stuffing, which can lead to search engine penalties and a poor user experience. Instead, aim for a keyword density of 1-3% and ensure the keywords flow seamlessly within your content.

4. Optimise your images:
   - Compress and resize images to reduce file sizes and improve page loading speed. Use descriptive filenames and alt text for your images, incorporating relevant keywords where appropriate. This helps search engines understand the context of your images and can boost your SEO performance.

5. Improve your site's loading speed:

- A fast-loading website is crucial for a positive user experience and better SEO rankings. Optimize your site's speed by enabling caching, using a content delivery network (CDN), and minimizing the use of plugins and scripts.
- Use tools like Google PageSpeed Insights or GTmetrix to analyse and improve your site's performance.

6. Create high-quality, engaging content:
   - Search engines prioritize high-quality, informative, and engaging content that provides value to users.
   - Focus on creating well-researched and well-written content that addresses your audience's needs and interests. This will encourage visitors to spend more time on your site, leading to lower bounce rates and higher search engine rankings.

7. Use internal and external links:
   - Incorporate internal links to other relevant content on your blog, guiding readers to additional resources and improving your site's overall navigation. Include external links to authoritative and credible sources to support your claims and enhance your content's credibility. This can help improve your SEO performance and demonstrate your expertise in your niche.

8. Optimize your URL structure:
   - Ensure your URLs are clear, concise, and keyword rich.
   - Use hyphens to separate words and avoid using special characters or numbers that may confuse search engines and users.
   - A well-structured URL can improve your search engine rankings and make it easier for users to understand the content of your page.

9. Implement schema markup:
   - Schema markup is a form of structured data that helps search engines understand your content and display it more effectively in search results.
   - Implementing schema markup can lead to rich snippets, which can improve click-through rates and increase your site's visibility.

10. Monitor your SEO performance:
   - Regularly track your site's SEO performance using tools like Google Analytics, Google Search Console, or other SEO analytics platforms.
   - This allows you to identify areas for improvement, monitor keyword rankings, and assess the effectiveness of your optimization efforts.

Promoting Your Blog to Grow Your Audience and Boost Engagement

Promoting your blog effectively is crucial for reaching a wider audience, increasing engagement, and growing your online presence. This guide will provide you with essential tips and strategies for promoting your blog across various channels and platforms, helping you attract more readers and achieve your blogging goals.

1. Leverage social media:
   - Create profiles for your blog on popular social media platforms such as Facebook, Twitter, Instagram, Pinterest, and LinkedIn.
   - Share your blog posts, engage with your followers, and participate in relevant groups or discussions to increase your blog's visibility and attract new readers.

2. Build an email list:
   - Offer an email subscription option on your blog, allowing visitors to receive updates and notifications when you publish updated content.
   - Use email marketing tools like Mailchimp or ConvertKit to manage your subscriber list and send out regular newsletters or promotional emails.

3. Network with other bloggers and influencers:
   - Connect with fellow digital nomad bloggers and influencers within your niche to build relationships, exchange ideas, and collaborate on projects or guest posts.
   - Engage with their content, leave thoughtful comments, and share their work on your social media channels to foster goodwill and mutual support.

4. Guest posting:
   - Offer to write high-quality guest posts for reputable blogs and websites within your niche. This not only exposes your content to a new audience but also helps establish your authority and credibility within the field.
   - Be sure to include a link back to your blog in your author bio or within the content, where appropriate.

5. Join online communities:
   - Participate in online forums, discussion boards, and communities related to your niche, such as Reddit, Quora, or niche-specific Facebook groups.
   - Share your expertise, answer questions, and provide valuable insights, while occasionally linking to relevant content on your blog.
   - Be genuine and helpful to avoid coming across as overly promotional.

6. Utilise content repurposing:
   - Transform your blog content into different formats, such as videos, podcasts, infographics, or slideshows, to reach a wider audience and cater to different content consumption preferences.
   - Share these repurposed content pieces on platforms like YouTube, Spotify, or SlideShare to attract new readers and drive traffic to your blog.

7. Collaborate on round-up posts:
   - Create round-up posts featuring insights, tips, or experiences from other digital nomads, influencers, or industry experts. These posts not only provide valuable content for your readers but also encourage featured contributors to share the post with their own followers, amplifying your reach.

8. Optimise your blog for SEO:
   - Ensure your blog content is optimized for search engines to increase organic traffic and visibility.
   - Follow best practices for keyword research, on-page optimization, and link building to improve your search engine rankings and attract more readers to your blog.

9. Run paid advertising campaigns:
   - Invest in paid advertising campaigns on platforms like Google Ads, Facebook Ads, or Instagram Ads to reach a targeted audience and drive traffic to your blog.
   - Experiment with different ad formats, targeting options, and budgets to find the most effective strategy for your goals.

10. Track and analyse your promotional efforts:
   - Use analytics tools like Google Analytics or social media analytics platforms to track the performance of your promotional efforts.
   - Analyse data such as traffic sources, engagement rates, and conversion metrics to identify which strategies are most effective and refine your approach accordingly.

Building an Email List to Connect with Your Audience and Boost Engagement

Building an email list is essential for maintaining a direct connection with your audience, promoting your content, and nurturing relationships with your readers. This guide will provide you with essential tips and strategies for growing your email list, helping you expand your reach and strengthen your blogging community.

1. Offer valuable incentives:
   - Entice your visitors to subscribe to your email list by offering exclusive content, free resources, or discounts in exchange for their email address.
   - Create valuable incentives such as eBooks, checklists, or guides that are relevant to your niche and provide tangible benefits to your readers.

2. Optimize your opt-in forms:
   - Design visually appealing opt-in forms that clearly communicate the benefits of subscribing to your email list.
   - Place these forms strategically throughout your blog, including in your sidebar, footer, within blog posts, or as a pop-up.
   - Use compelling language and strong call-to-actions to encourage visitors to sign up.

3. Create a dedicated landing page:
   - Design a dedicated landing page specifically for email sign-ups, highlighting the benefits of joining your email list and featuring a prominent opt-in form.
   - Share this landing page on your social media profiles, in your blog posts, or within your guest posts on other websites to drive traffic and encourage subscriptions.

4. Utilize content upgrades:
   - Offer content upgrades within your blog posts, such as additional resources, templates, or bonus material related to the post's topic. These upgrades are accessible only to those who provide their email address, encouraging subscriptions from readers already engaged with your content.

5. Run contests and giveaways:
   - Host contests or giveaways on your blog or social media platforms, requiring participants to subscribe to your email list as a condition for entry.
   - Choose prizes that are relevant to your niche and appealing to your target audience and promote the contest widely to maximise participation.

6. Leverage social media:
   - Promote your email list and incentives on your social media channels to attract new subscribers from your existing followers.
   - Share links to your dedicated landing page, highlight the benefits of subscribing, and engage with your audience to create excitement around your email list.

11. Use exit-intent pop-ups:
    - Implement exit-intent pop-ups that display an opt-in form when a visitor is about to leave your site. This provides a final opportunity to capture their email address before they exit, increasing your chances of growing your email list.

12. Collaborate with other bloggers or influencers:
    - Partner with other bloggers or influencers within your niche to co-create content or host joint giveaways, encouraging their audience to subscribe to your email list. This exposes your blog to a new audience and can help grow your email list quickly.

13. Prioritize email list segmentation:
    - Segment your email list based on factors such as demographics, interests, or engagement levels to deliver more targeted and relevant content to your subscribers. This not only increases open rates and engagement but also helps prevent unsubscribes by providing content that truly resonates with your audience.

14. Monitor and analyse your list growth:
    - Track the performance of your email list growth strategies using tools like Google Analytics or your email marketing platform's analytics features.
    - Analyse key metrics such as subscription rates, open rates, and click-through rates to identify which strategies are most effective and refine your approach accordingly.

Monetising Your Blog to Generate Sustainable Income While Travelling

Monetizing your blog is crucial for generating a sustainable income that supports your traveling lifestyle. This guide will provide you with essential tips and strategies for monetizing your blog through various channels, helping you achieve financial independence and the freedom to explore the world.

1. Affiliate marketing:
   - Promote products or services from other companies within your niche and earn a commission for every sale made through your unique referral link.
   - Join affiliate programs such as Amazon Associates, ShareASale, or Commission Junction, and choose products that align with your blog's content and audience interests.

2. Sponsored posts:
   - Partner with brands or companies to create sponsored content featuring their products or services.
   - Ensure that sponsored posts are relevant to your niche, provide value to your audience, and adhere to disclosure guidelines set forth by the Federal Trade Commission (FTC).

3. Display advertising:
   - Place banner ads or other display advertisements on your blog to generate revenue through pay-per-click (PPC) or pay-per-impression (CPM) models.
   - Join ad networks like Google AdSense, Media.net, or Ezoic to gain access to advertisers and easily manage your ad placements.

4. Sell digital products:

- Create and sell digital products such as eBooks, courses, templates, or printables related to your niche. These products can be sold directly through your blog or via platforms like Gumroad, Teachable, or Etsy, providing your audience with valuable resources and generating passive income.

5. Offer consulting or coaching services:
   - Leverage your expertise within your niche to offer consulting or coaching services to your audience.
   - Provide personalized advice, guidance, or mentoring to clients, helping them achieve their goals or overcome challenges related to your niche.

6. Host webinars or workshops:
   - Organize webinars or online workshops on topics relevant to your niche, charging attendees a fee to participate.
   - Share valuable insights, tips, or skills during these events, and offer additional resources or support to attendees after the event.

7. Create a membership site:
   - Develop a membership site or offer premium content available only to paying subscribers. This can include exclusive articles, videos, resources, or access to a private community where members can interact with you and one another.

8. Sell physical products:
   - Design and sell physical products such as branded merchandise, travel accessories, or niche-specific items through your blog.
   - Use platforms like Shopify, WooCommerce, or Printful to manage your online store and handle order fulfilment.

9. Write sponsored reviews:
   - Collaborate with companies to write sponsored reviews of their products or services, earning a fee for your honest and detailed evaluation.
   - Ensure the products or services are relevant to your niche and that you maintain transparency with your audience by disclosing the sponsored nature of the review.

10. Offer freelance services:
    - Promote your skills as a writer, photographer, graphic designer, or social media manager, and offer freelance services to clients through your blog.

11. Showcase your portfolio and client testimonials to establish credibility and attract potential clients.

Analysing and Improving Your Blog for Continued Growth and Success

Regularly analysing and improving your blog is essential for sustaining growth, increasing engagement, and maintaining relevance within your niche. This guide will provide you with essential tips and strategies for evaluating your blog's performance and implementing changes to optimize your content, design, and overall user experience.

1. Set measurable goals and objectives:
   - Establish clear, measurable goals and objectives for your blog, such as increasing traffic, boosting engagement, or growing your email list.

- These goals will provide a framework for analysing your blog's performance and identifying areas for improvement.

2. Monitor key performance metrics:
   - Use analytics tools like Google Analytics, Google Search Console, or your email marketing platform's analytics features to track key performance metrics, such as page views, bounce rate, session duration, and conversion rates.
   - Regularly monitoring these metrics will help you gauge your blog's performance and identify trends or potential issues.

3. Conduct content audits:
   - Periodically review your blog content to ensure it remains relevant, accurate, and up to date.
   - Identify underperforming or outdated content and revise or update it as needed, incorporating SEO best practices, and addressing any gaps or inconsistencies in your content strategy.

4. Optimize your site for SEO:
   - Analyse your blog's SEO performance using tools like SEMrush, Ahrefs, or Moz to identify areas for improvement.
   - Optimize your content, meta tags, URL structure, and internal linking to improve your search engine rankings and attract more organic traffic.

5. Evaluate your blog design and user experience:
   - Regularly assess your blog's design, layout, and overall user experience.
   - Ensure your site is visually appealing, easy to navigate, and responsive on all devices. Use tools like Google PageSpeed Insights or GTmetrix to analyse your site's loading speed and implement improvements as needed.

6. Gather user feedback:
   - Collect feedback from your audience through surveys, polls, or direct communication to gain insights into their needs, preferences, and pain points.
   - Use this feedback to inform your content strategy, improve your blog's user experience, and address any issues or concerns raised by your readers.

7. Test different monetization strategies:
   - Experiment with various monetization methods, such as affiliate marketing, display advertising, or selling digital products, to determine which strategies are most effective for generating income through your blog.
   - Continuously optimize and refine your monetization approach based on your audience's preferences and your blog's performance.

8. Engage with your audience:
   - Interact with your readers through blog comments, social media, or your email newsletter to build relationships, encourage feedback, and gain insights into their needs and interests.
   - Use this information to create content that resonates with your audience and drives engagement.

9. Stay informed about industry trends and best practices:

- Keep up to date with the latest trends and best practices within your niche and the blogging world by reading industry news, attending conferences or webinars, and networking with other bloggers. This will help you stay ahead of the curve and maintain relevance within your niche.

10. Iterate and adapt:
- Continuously analyse your blog's performance, implement improvements, and adapt your strategies based on your findings and feedback from your audience.
- Embrace a growth mindset and be open to change, recognizing that your blog's success depends on your ability to learn, evolve, and adapt to the ever-changing digital landscape.

AFFILIATE MARKETING

Affiliate marketing is an increasingly popular online revenue generation strategy that benefits both businesses and individuals. In this short article, we will explain the basics of affiliate marketing, how it works, and why it is an attractive option for online entrepreneurs.

What is Affiliate Marketing?

Affiliate marketing is a performance-based marketing strategy where businesses partner with individuals (affiliates) to promote their products or services. In return, affiliates receive a commission for each sale or lead generated through their unique referral links or promotional efforts. This win-win situation allows businesses to expand their reach, while affiliates can earn a passive income without creating or managing their own products or services.

How Does Affiliate Marketing Work?

The affiliate marketing process typically involves three key players: the merchant, the affiliate, and the customer. Here is a brief overview of the steps involved:

- Merchants create an affiliate program, offering commissions to individuals who help promote their products or services.
- Affiliates sign up for the program and receive unique referral links or promotional materials.
- Affiliates share these links or materials through their websites, social media platforms, email campaigns, or other channels to reach potential customers.
- Customers click on the affiliate links, which directs them to the merchant's website.
- If the customer makes a purchase or completes the desired action (e.g., signing up for a newsletter), the affiliate receives a commission for their referral.

Why is Affiliate Marketing Attractive to Digital Nomads?

Affiliate marketing is an appealing option for online entrepreneurs for several reasons:

1. Low start-up costs:
   - Unlike starting a traditional business, affiliate marketing requires minimal upfront investment.
   - Affiliates need only a website, social media presence, or other online platforms to start promoting products and services.

2. Passive income potential:
   - Once affiliates have established their marketing channels, they can generate income without actively managing the process, allowing them to focus on other projects or enjoy more leisure time.

3. Flexibility and scalability:
   - Affiliates can work from anywhere and promote products in various niches, adjusting their marketing strategies as needed to maximize revenue.

4. No inventory or customer service required:
   - Affiliates do not have to worry about product creation, inventory management, or customer support, as the merchant handles these responsibilities.

Affiliate marketing offers digital nomads an excellent opportunity to generate passive income while traveling the world. This guide will provide an overview of the steps you need to take to become a successful affiliate marketer as a digital nomad.

Choose Your Niche

As a digital nomad, it is essential to select a niche that aligns with your interests and expertise. Focusing on a specific niche allows you to establish yourself as an authority and target a well-defined audience. Consider niches related to travel, remote work, or lifestyle topics that cater to your firsthand experiences and resonate with your target audience.

Build Your Online Presence

To succeed in affiliate marketing, you need a platform to promote products and services. Create a website or blog, start a YouTube channel, or grow your social media presence on platforms like Instagram, Facebook, or Twitter. Focus on creating high-quality content that offers value to your audience and establishes trust.

Join Affiliate Programs

Research and join relevant affiliate programs in your chosen niche. Popular affiliate networks like Amazon Associates, ShareASale, and CJ Affiliate offer a wide range of products and services to promote. Alternatively, seek out independent affiliate programs offered by companies in your niche. Always evaluate commission structures, payment terms, and promotional resources before joining a program.

Create Engaging Content

Consistently produce valuable and engaging content that resonates with your target audience. Consider writing blog posts, creating videos, or sharing social media posts that incorporate affiliate links naturally. Focus on providing helpful information, tutorials, product reviews, or recommendations that solve problems or answer questions for your audience.

Optimize for SEO

To attract organic traffic, optimize your content for search engines by conducting keyword research, using relevant keywords in your titles and content, and ensuring your site is mobile-friendly. Utilize SEO tools like Google Analytics, Ahrefs, or Moz to monitor your site's performance and adjust your strategies accordingly.

Promote Your Content

Share your content across multiple channels, including social media, email newsletters, and online communities or forums relevant to your niche. Engage with your audience, respond to comments, and build relationships to establish trust and encourage sharing.

Track and Analyse Your Performance

Monitor your affiliate marketing performance using analytics tools provided by your affiliate programs or third-party solutions like Google Analytics. Analyse your data to identify which content and promotional strategies are driving conversions and adjust your approach to maximize your earnings.

Network with Fellow Digital Nomads

Connect with other digital nomads involved in affiliate marketing to share experiences, learn from their successes and mistakes, and explore potential collaboration opportunities. Engage in online communities, attend digital nomad meetups, or join mastermind groups to expand your network and knowledge.

Diversify Your Income Streams

As you become more experienced in affiliate marketing, consider diversifying your income streams by joining additional affiliate programs, promoting distinct types of products, or expanding into new niches. This will help mitigate risks associated with relying on a sole source of income.

ONLINE TUTORING

Becoming an online tutor is an excellent opportunity for those looking to share their knowledge and earn an income while enjoying a flexible schedule. Freelance tutors can set their working hours and charge competitive rates based on experience and specialization. In this comprehensive guide, we will walk you through the process of becoming a successful online tutor, from choosing your subject area to finding clients and growing your tutoring business.

Identifying Your Subject Area

It is crucial to identify a subject area that aligns with your expertise, interests, and the needs of your target audience. This guide will provide you with essential tips and strategies for selecting the perfect subject area and setting the foundation for a successful online tutoring career.

1. Assess your strengths and expertise:
   - Begin by evaluating your academic background, professional experience, and personal interests to identify the subjects you are most knowledgeable and passionate about.
   - Consider your qualifications, certifications, or any specialized training you have received that could set you apart as an expert in a specific subject.

2. Determine your target audience:
   - Think about the age group and learning needs of the students you would like to work with, such as elementary school children, high school students, college students, or adults.
   - Different age groups and learning levels require different approaches and teaching styles, so consider your preferences and strengths when selecting your target audience.

3. Research market demand:
   - Conduct market research to determine the demand for various subject areas within your target audience.
   - Some subjects, such as math, science, and language learning, tend to have a higher demand for tutors. Investigate the popularity of different subjects in online tutoring platforms, forums, or social media groups to gauge the market's needs.

4. Identify your niche:
   - Narrow down your subject area by identifying a specific niche that aligns with your expertise, interests, and market demand.
   - Focusing on a niche allows you to cater to a specific segment of the market and establish yourself as a specialized expert, setting you apart from competitors.

5. Analyse the competition:
   - Research other online tutors in your chosen subject area to identify their strengths, weaknesses, and unique selling points.
   - Determine how you can differentiate yourself from the competition by offering a unique approach, focusing on a specific niche, or providing additional resources or support.

6. Create a unique selling proposition (USP):
   - Develop a USP that highlights your strengths, expertise, and the unique benefits you provide as an online tutor in your chosen subject area.
   - Your USP will serve as a foundation for marketing your services and attracting potential clients.

7. Test your subject area with a pilot program:
   - Before fully committing to your chosen subject area, consider offering a pilot program or free trial lessons to test the market's response. This will give you valuable feedback and insights into the effectiveness of your teaching methods and help you refine your approach before fully launching your online tutoring business.

8. Continuously update your knowledge and skills:
   - To remain relevant and competitive as an online tutor, it is essential to stay up to date with the latest developments, trends, and best practices within your subject area.

- Regularly attend workshops, webinars, or conferences, and engage with industry news and resources to maintain your expertise and credibility.

Assess Your Qualifications and Skills:

It is essential to assess your qualifications and skills to ensure you are well-prepared for your new venture. This guide will provide you with essential tips and strategies for evaluating your qualifications, identifying your strengths, and developing the necessary skills to excel in the world of online tutoring.

1. Review your educational background:
   - Examine your academic credentials, including any degrees, certifications, or diplomas you have earned.
   - Consider how these qualifications relate to the subject area you have chosen for tutoring and whether they provide a solid foundation for teaching others.

2. Evaluate your professional experience:
   - Assess your work history and identify any experiences that align with your chosen subject area or demonstrate your ability to teach and communicate effectively.
   - Consider any roles where you have trained, mentored, or taught others, as these experiences can help demonstrate your skills as a tutor.

3. Identify your subject matter expertise:
   - Reflect on your knowledge and expertise in your chosen subject area.
   - Determine whether you have a deep understanding of the subject matter and can break down complex concepts into easy-to-understand lessons for your students.

4. Assess your teaching skills:
   - Evaluate your ability to communicate complex ideas effectively, adapt your teaching style to different learning needs, and create engaging lesson plans.
   - Reflect on any past teaching experiences or seek feedback from friends or family members to gauge your aptitude for teaching.

5. Determine your technical skills:
   - As an online tutor, it is crucial to have strong technical skills, including proficiency in using video conferencing tools, online whiteboards, and document-sharing platforms.
   - Evaluate your familiarity and comfort level with these technologies and invest time in learning any necessary tools.

6. Identify areas for improvement:
   - Once you have assessed your qualifications and skills, identify any gaps or areas for improvement.
   - This might include obtaining additional certifications, enhancing your subject matter knowledge, or developing your teaching or technical skills.

7. Pursue relevant certifications or training:
   - If your qualifications need bolstering, consider pursuing relevant certifications, degrees, or training programs that will strengthen your credibility and expertise as an online tutor.
   - Research reputable institutions or online platforms that offer courses or certifications in your subject area or teaching methodologies.

8. Develop your teaching skills:
   - If you are new to teaching or looking to enhance your skills, consider taking courses in teaching methodologies, learning styles, or classroom management.
   - Joining a teaching community, attending workshops, or seeking mentorship from experienced tutors can also help improve your teaching skills.

9. Expand your technical skills:
   - Invest time in learning and mastering the tools and technologies commonly used in online tutoring.
   - Familiarize yourself with video conferencing platforms, screen sharing tools, and online whiteboards to ensure a seamless and professional online tutoring experience for your students.

10. Continuously reassess and grow:
    - As you gain experience as an online tutor, continually reassess your qualifications and skills to identify areas for improvement.
    - Commit to lifelong learning and professional development to ensure you remain a highly qualified and effective tutor.

Choosing the Right Tutoring Platform

Selecting the right tutoring platform is crucial for reaching your target audience and providing a seamless learning experience. This guide will provide you with essential tips and strategies for choosing the perfect tutoring platform that aligns with your needs, skills, and subject area.

1. Research popular tutoring platforms:
   - Start by researching popular online tutoring platforms such as VIPKid, Chegg, Tutor.com, Wyzant, or Preply.
   - Read reviews, gather information about their subject offerings, target audience, and pricing models to understand how each platform operates and caters to tutors and students.

2. Assess the platform's reputation and credibility:
   - Choose a platform with a formidable reputation and credibility among both tutors and students.
   - Look for platforms with positive reviews, testimonials, and a history of success in connecting tutors with students.
   - A platform with a solid reputation will help you attract more clients and build trust with potential students.

3. Determine the target audience and subject offerings:
   - Select a platform that caters to your target audience and offers tutoring opportunities in your subject area.
   - Some platforms may focus on specific age groups, such as K-12 students or adult learners, while others may cater to a broader audience.
   - Ensure that the platform you choose aligns with your expertise and target market.

4. Evaluate the platform's user interface and features:
   - Choose a tutoring platform that offers a user-friendly interface and features that facilitate seamless online tutoring.

- Look for platforms with built-in video conferencing, screen sharing, online whiteboards, and document-sharing capabilities.
- These tools will help you create an engaging and interactive learning experience for your students.

5. Consider the platform's pricing model and commission fees:
   - Different tutoring platforms have varying pricing models and commission structures.
   - Some platforms may charge a flat fee or take a percentage of your earnings, while others may require tutors to purchase tokens or pay for visibility.
   - Compare the pricing models and commission fees across different platforms to find one that aligns with your financial goals and expectations.

6. Evaluate the platform's support and resources for tutors:
   - Choose a platform that offers comprehensive support and resources for tutors, such as training materials, lesson plan templates, or access to a community of fellow tutors.
   - These resources can help you improve your teaching skills, streamline your lesson planning process, and connect with other professionals in your field.

7. Assess the platform's policies and guidelines:
   - Review the platform's policies and guidelines, such as tutor qualifications, student-tutor interactions, and dispute resolution processes.
   - Ensure that the platform's policies align with your values and expectations as an online tutor.

8. Test the platform with a trial period: Before fully committing to a tutoring platform, consider signing up for a trial period or offering a limited number of lessons to test the platform's features, user experience, and student base. This will help you determine whether the platform is a good fit for your needs and teaching style.

9. Continuously reassess your choice: As you gain experience as an online tutor, continually reassess the performance and suitability of your chosen platform. Be open to exploring other platforms or adjusting your tutoring approach to optimize your success and the experience of your students.

Setting Your Rates

Setting appropriate rates is crucial for attracting clients and generating a sustainable income. This guide will provide you with essential tips and strategies for determining your rates, considering factors such as your qualifications, experience, and market demand.

1. Assess your qualifications and experience:
   - Begin by evaluating your qualifications, certifications, and professional experience in your chosen subject area.
   - Tutors with higher levels of education, specialised certifications, or extensive experience can typically charge higher rates.

2. Research market rates:
   - Conduct market research to determine the average hourly rates for online tutors in your subject area and target audience.
   - Browse tutoring platforms, forums, or social media groups to gather information on the rates charged by tutors with similar qualifications and experience.

3. Consider your target audience:
   - Keep in mind the financial capabilities of your target audience when setting your rates. For example, if you are targeting high school students, your rates may need to be more affordable compared to tutoring college students or working professionals.

4. Factor in your expenses:
   - As a digital nomad, consider the costs associated with your lifestyle and online tutoring, such as internet fees, equipment, marketing expenses, and any platform fees or commissions. Your rates should cover these costs while providing you with a fair income.

5. Determine your desired hourly income:
   - Calculate your desired hourly income based on your financial goals, considering your living expenses, savings goals, and any taxes or fees applicable to your earnings. This will help you establish a baseline for your tutoring rates.

6. Offer pricing tiers or packages:
   - Consider offering pricing tiers or lesson packages to provide clients with more flexibility and options. For example, you could offer discounted rates for purchasing a certain number of lessons upfront or provide different tiers based on lesson duration, level of support, or additional resources.

7. Be prepared to negotiate:
   - Some clients may request a lower rate or a discount. Be prepared to negotiate your rates within reason, but also know your worth and set a minimum rate with which you are comfortable.

8. Test your rates and adjust as needed:
   - Start with a rate that you believe is fair based on your research and personal goals, then adjust as needed based on market response and feedback from clients.
   - It is essential to remain flexible and open to making changes as you gain more experience and better understand your value in the market.

9. Regularly review and update your rates:
   - As your experience, qualifications, and market demand evolve, periodically review, and update your rates to ensure they remain competitive and accurately reflect your value as an online tutor.

Developing a Teaching Plan

Having a well-structured teaching plan is crucial for delivering effective and engaging lessons. This guide will provide you with essential tips and strategies for developing a teaching plan that meets the needs of your students, enhances their learning experience, and sets you apart as a professional online tutor.

1. Understand your students' needs:
   - Begin by assessing the learning needs, goals, and preferences of your students.
   - Gather information through initial consultations, questionnaires, or feedback from previous lessons. Understanding your students' needs will help you tailor your teaching plan to their unique requirements.

2. Set clear objectives:
   - Define clear, measurable objectives for each lesson or series of lessons.
   - These objectives should align with your students' goals and serve as a roadmap for their learning progress.
   - Establishing clear objectives also helps you maintain focus and structure during lessons.

3. Break down complex concepts:
   - Identify the key concepts and topics within your subject area and break them down into smaller, manageable segments.
   - This will help you organize your teaching plan and ensure that your students can easily grasp and build upon the material.

4. Create engaging and interactive lessons:
   - Incorporate various teaching methods and activities into your lessons to keep your students engaged and cater to different learning styles.
   - Use a mix of lectures, discussions, problem-solving activities, and multimedia resources to create a dynamic and interactive learning experience.

5. Develop assessment methods:
   - Establish assessment methods to evaluate your students' progress and understanding of the material. This may include quizzes, assignments, presentations, or informal assessments during lessons.
   - Regular assessments help you identify areas where your students may need additional support or guidance.

6. Plan for feedback and reflection:
   - Incorporate opportunities for feedback and reflection into your teaching plan.
   - Encourage students to ask questions, share their thoughts, and discuss their learning progress.
   - Regularly provide constructive feedback to help students improve and stay motivated.

7. Establish a clear lesson structure:
   - Organize your lessons with a clear structure that includes an introduction, main content, and conclusion. This will help you maintain a consistent and organized approach while guiding your students through the learning process.

8. Adapt your teaching plan as needed:
   - Be prepared to adapt your teaching plan based on your students' progress, feedback, or changes in their goals.
   - Continuously assess and adjust your plan to ensure it remains relevant and effective for each student's unique needs.

9. Continuously update your teaching plan:
   - As a subject matter expert, it is essential to stay up to date with the latest developments, trends, and best practices in your field.
   - Regularly revise and update your teaching plan to incorporate current information and ensure your students receive the most current and relevant instruction.

10. Utilize technology and online resources:

- Leverage technology and online resources to enhance your teaching plan and facilitate a seamless learning experience.
- Familiarize yourself with video conferencing platforms, online whiteboards, and document-sharing tools to support your students' learning and collaboration.

Marketing Your Tutoring Services:

Effectively marketing your services is crucial for attracting clients and establishing a successful tutoring business. This guide will provide you with essential tips and strategies for promoting your tutoring services, building your brand, and reaching your target audience.

1. Create a professional online presence:
   - Establish a professional online presence by creating a website or portfolio showcasing your qualifications, experience, and areas of expertise.
   - Include client testimonials, sample lesson plans, and a clear call-to-action for potential clients to contact you.

2. Utilize social media platforms:
   - Leverage social media platforms like Facebook, LinkedIn, Instagram, and Twitter to reach a wider audience and engage with potential clients.
   - Share educational content, tips, and updates about your tutoring services to showcase your expertise and connect with your target audience.

3. Join online tutoring platforms:
   - Sign up for popular online tutoring platforms like VIPKid, Chegg, Tutor.com, Wyzant, or Preply to increase your visibility and credibility among potential clients. These platforms can help you connect with students looking for tutoring services in your subject area.

4. Network with fellow tutors and educators:
   - Connect with fellow tutors, educators, and professionals in your subject area through online forums, social media groups, and networking events.
   - Building relationships with others in your field can lead to referrals, collaboration opportunities, and valuable insights into marketing strategies.

5. Offer free or discounted trial sessions:
   - Attract new clients by offering free or discounted trial sessions. This allows potential clients to experience your teaching style and assess the quality of your tutoring services before committing to a full-priced lesson or package.

6. Collaborate with educational institutions or organizations:
   - Partner with local schools, universities, or educational organizations to offer your tutoring services to their students. This can help you gain access to a larger pool of potential clients and establish credibility within your target market.

7. Optimize your website for search engines (SEO):
   - Invest time in optimizing your website for search engines by incorporating relevant keywords, creating valuable content, and building high-quality backlinks.
   - Effective SEO can help improve your website's visibility and attract potential clients searching for tutoring services in your subject area.

8. Utilize content marketing strategies:
   - Create and share valuable content, such as blog posts, articles, videos, or podcasts, to showcase your expertise and engage with your target audience.
   - Content marketing can help you establish yourself as an authority in your subject area and attract potential clients.

9. Collect and showcase testimonials:
   - Gather testimonials from satisfied clients and showcase them on your website and social media profiles.
   - Positive reviews and testimonials can help build trust with potential clients and demonstrate the value of your tutoring services.

10. Monitor and adjust your marketing strategies:
   - Regularly assess the effectiveness of your marketing strategies and adjust as needed to optimize your results.
   - Track your website traffic, social media engagement, and client inquiries to identify which strategies are driving the best results.

Maintaining a Professional and Engaging Online Environment

creating and maintaining a professional and engaging online environment is crucial for ensuring effective learning experiences and building trust with your students. This guide will provide you with essential tips and strategies for fostering a conducive online learning environment that keeps your students motivated and focused.

1. Set clear expectations and guidelines:
   - At the beginning of each tutoring relationship, establish clear expectations and guidelines regarding communication, behaviour, and lesson objectives. This will help create a structured learning environment and ensure that both you and your students understand the ground rules.

2. Invest in reliable technology:
   - Ensure that you have a stable internet connection, high-quality audio and video equipment, and a quiet workspace to conduct your online tutoring sessions. Reliable technology is essential for creating a professional online environment and minimizing disruptions during lessons.

3. Utilize interactive teaching tools:
   - Leverage interactive teaching tools such as online whiteboards, screen sharing, and multimedia resources to create an engaging learning experience for your students. These tools can help facilitate collaboration, communication, and understanding of complex concepts.

4. Maintain a professional appearance:
   - Dress professionally and ensure that your workspace is clean and organized during online tutoring sessions. Maintaining a professional appearance helps establish credibility and sets a positive tone for the learning environment.

5. Encourage open communication and feedback:
   - Foster an environment where students feel comfortable asking questions, sharing their thoughts, and providing feedback on their learning experience.

- Encourage open communication and actively listen to your students' concerns to create a supportive and collaborative atmosphere.

6. Be punctual and organized:
   - Arrive on time for each tutoring session and have your lesson materials and teaching plan ready to go. Demonstrating punctuality and organization shows your students that you take your role as a tutor seriously and respect their time.

7. Be patient and empathetic:
   - Understand that each student learns at their own pace and may face unique challenges in grasping certain concepts. Be patient and empathetic, offering guidance and encouragement when needed to create a positive and supportive learning environment.

8. Continuously improve your teaching skills:
   - Invest in your professional development by attending workshops, webinars, or conferences related to online tutoring or your subject area.
   - Continuously improving your teaching skills will help you create a more engaging and effective learning environment for your students.

9. Monitor student progress and adjust your teaching plan:
   - Regularly assess your students' progress and adjust your teaching plan as needed to address any challenges or gaps in understanding.
   - Adapting your teaching plan based on your students' needs helps maintain an engaging and supportive learning environment.

10. Celebrate achievements and milestones:
    - Acknowledge and celebrate your students' achievements and milestones, no matter how small. Positive reinforcement can boost motivation and keep students engaged in their learning journey.

Continuously Improving Your Skills

Continuous improvement of your skills is essential for staying competitive and providing top-notch tutoring services to your students. This guide will provide you with essential tips and strategies for enhancing your subject matter expertise, teaching abilities, and professional development as an online tutor.

1. Stay up to date with industry trends and developments:
   - Regularly read articles, journals, and books related to your subject area and the education industry to stay informed about the latest trends and developments.
   - Staying up to date ensures that your knowledge remains current and relevant for your students.

2. Participate in professional development courses:
   - Enrol in professional development courses or workshops related to your subject area, teaching methodologies, or technology used in online tutoring.
   - Expanding your skill set will help you become a more effective tutor and stand out from the competition.

3. Attend conferences and webinars:

- Participate in industry conferences, webinars, or networking events to learn from other professionals in the field and stay informed about best practices and emerging trends.
- Networking with other educators can provide valuable insights and resources for your own tutoring practice.

4. Collaborate with fellow tutors and educators:
   - Connect with other tutors and educators to exchange ideas, strategies, and resources. Collaboration can lead to new insights and opportunities for growth, as well as help you stay motivated and engaged in your professional development.

5. Reflect on your teaching practice:
   - Regularly reflect on your teaching methods, student feedback, and the outcomes of your tutoring sessions.
   - Identify areas where you can improve and implement changes to enhance your effectiveness as an online tutor.

6. Seek feedback from students and peers:
   - Request feedback from your students and fellow tutors to gain insight into your strengths and areas for improvement.
   - Constructive feedback can help you refine your teaching methods and continuously improve your skills.

7. Experiment with new teaching methods and tools:
   - Stay open to trying new teaching methods, technologies, and tools to enhance your tutoring sessions.
   - Experimentation can lead to more engaging and effective learning experiences for your students.

8. Set professional development goals:
   - Establish clear, measurable goals for your professional development as an online tutor. These goals can help you stay focused on continuous improvement and provide motivation for ongoing learning and growth.

9. Monitor your progress:
   - Regularly assess your progress towards your professional development goals and adjust your strategies as needed.
   - Monitoring your progress can help you stay on track and ensure that you are making meaningful improvements in your skills and expertise.

10. Join professional associations and organizations:
    - Consider joining professional associations and organizations related to your subject area or the education industry.
    - Membership in these organizations can provide access to valuable resources, networking opportunities, and professional development events.

Collecting Feedback and Testimonials:

Collecting feedback and testimonials from students is crucial for assessing your performance, refining your teaching methods, and building credibility. This guide will provide you with essential tips and strategies for effectively gathering feedback and testimonials from your students.

1. Establish a feedback culture:
   - From the beginning of your tutoring relationship, foster a culture of open communication and feedback with your students.
   - Encourage them to share their thoughts, questions, and concerns about their learning experience to create a supportive and collaborative environment.

2. Use various feedback methods:
   - Utilize various methods for collecting feedback, such as in-session discussions, email surveys, or anonymous feedback forms.
   - Offering multiple channels for feedback can help you gather a wider range of perspectives and insights.

3. Ask for feedback regularly:
   - Request feedback from your students at regular intervals, such as after each lesson or at the end of a unit.
   - Consistent feedback collection can help you identify trends, monitor progress, and make timely adjustments to your teaching methods.

4. Be specific with your feedback requests:
   - When asking for feedback, provide specific prompts or questions that guide your students to focus on aspects of your tutoring sessions. This can help you gather more actionable insights and make targeted improvements.

5. Create a safe space for honest feedback:
   - Encourage your students to provide honest and constructive feedback by creating a safe and non-judgmental space for communication.
   - Reassure them that their opinions are valued and that their feedback will be used to enhance their learning experience.

6. Act on the feedback you receive:
   - Demonstrate to your students that you take their feedback seriously by implementing changes based on their suggestions. This not only helps you improve as a tutor but also builds trust with your students and encourages them to continue providing feedback.

7. Request testimonials from satisfied students:
   - Ask satisfied students if they would be willing to provide a written or video testimonial about their experience with your tutoring services.
   - Be sure to obtain their permission before sharing their testimonials publicly.

8. Showcase your testimonials:
   - Display your students' testimonials prominently on your website, social media profiles, and marketing materials.
   - Positive reviews can help build credibility and trust with potential clients, demonstrating the value of your tutoring services.

9. Analyse feedback for trends and patterns:
   - Regularly review the feedback you receive from your students to identify trends, patterns, and areas for improvement.
   - This can help you pinpoint specific aspects of your tutoring practice that require attention and guide your professional development efforts.

10. Express gratitude for feedback and testimonials:
   - Always thank your students for taking the time to provide feedback and testimonials. Expressing gratitude reinforces the value of their input and encourages them to continue sharing their thoughts and experiences.

Expanding Your Services:

Expanding your services can help you increase your income, reach a wider audience, and stay competitive in the market. This guide will provide you with essential tips and strategies for diversifying your offerings and growing your online tutoring business.

1. Identify complementary subject areas:
   - Assess your expertise and consider offering tutoring services in related subject areas.
   - Expanding your subject matter expertise can help you attract a more diverse range of students and increase your earning potential.

2. Offer group tutoring sessions:
   - In addition to one-on-one tutoring, consider offering group tutoring sessions for students with similar needs or interests.
   - Group sessions can help you reach more students at once, maximize your time, and increase your income.

3. Develop specialized courses or workshops:
   - Create specialized courses or workshops focused on specific topics or skills within your subject area. These offerings can help you attract students seeking targeted learning experiences and set you apart from other tutors.

4. Offer tutoring packages or subscriptions:
   - Develop tutoring packages or subscription plans that provide students with a set number of sessions or access to ongoing support for a fixed price. This can encourage long-term commitment from students and provide you with a more predictable income stream.

5. Create and sell educational resources:
   - Develop educational materials, such as e-books, worksheets, or lesson plans, which complement your tutoring services. Selling these resources can provide an additional income stream and help you establish yourself as an authority in your subject area.

6. Offer consulting or coaching services:
   - Leverage your expertise to offer consulting or coaching services to parents, schools, or organizations. This can help you diversify your income sources and broaden your professional network.

7. Provide test preparation services:
   - Offer specialized tutoring services for students preparing for standardized tests, such as the SAT, ACT, or GRE. Test preparation is a high-demand area in the tutoring industry and can help you attract more clients.

8. Explore corporate training opportunities:
   - Consider offering your expertise to businesses or organizations seeking training in your subject area. Corporate training can provide a lucrative income stream and help you build valuable connections in your industry.

9. Offer language tutoring or conversation practice:
   - If you are fluent in more than one language, consider offering language tutoring or conversation practice services. Language learning is in high demand, and your skills can help you reach a global audience.

10. Collaborate with other tutors or educators:
    - Form partnerships with other tutors or educators to create joint offerings, such as multi-disciplinary courses or workshops. Collaboration can help you expand your services, reach new audiences, and learn from other professionals in your field.

FREELANCE WRITING

Working as a freelance writer offers flexibility, creative freedom, and a chance to hone your skills while earning a living.

This comprehensive guide will walk you through the necessary steps to find success in creating content for various clients.

Assessing your skills and interests

Identifying your skills and interests is the first step to finding your niche and building a successful business. This guide will provide you with essential tips and strategies for assessing your writing abilities, interests, and expertise to set the foundation for your freelance writing career.

1. Evaluate your writing skills:
   - Take an honest look at your writing abilities, considering factors such as grammar, style, and creativity.
   - Identify your strengths and areas for improvement to better understand your skillset and potential as a freelance writer.

2. Reflect on your interests:
   - Make a list of topics and industries that genuinely interest you.
   - Pursuing writing projects in areas that you are passionate about can lead to higher-quality work, increased motivation, and greater job satisfaction.

3. Identify your expertise:

- Consider your educational background, professional experience, and personal knowledge when identifying areas of expertise.
- Leveraging your expertise in specific subject matters can help you stand out as an authority in your niche and attract clients seeking specialized content.

4. Analyse your past writing experiences:
   - Reflect on previous writing experiences, including academic papers, blog posts, or professional projects.
   - Analyse these experiences to identify the types of writing you enjoy and excel at, such as long-form articles, technical writing, or creative storytelling.

5. Research industry trends and demand:
   - Investigate the current trends and demands in the freelance writing market to identify potential niches that align with your skills and interests.
   - Understanding the market can help you make informed decisions about the types of writing services to offer and the industries to target.

6. Experiment with different writing styles and formats:
   - Try your hand at various writing styles and formats, such as blog posts, whitepapers, or social media content, to discover which types of writing projects you enjoy and are most proficient at.

7. Seek feedback from peers and mentors:
   - Share your writing samples with peers, mentors, or professionals in the writing industry to gain valuable feedback on your work.
   - Constructive criticism can help you identify your strengths and areas for improvement, guiding your skill development and specialization.

8. Assess your adaptability:
   - Consider your ability to adapt to different writing styles, tones, and subject matters. As a freelance writer, being versatile and adaptable can open up more opportunities and help you succeed in a competitive market.

9. Set realistic goals:
   - Based on your assessment of your skills, interests, and expertise, set realistic goals for your freelance writing career.
   - Establishing clear objectives can help you stay focused on your professional development and guide your decisions about the projects you take on.

10. Continuously reassess and refine your niche:
    - As you gain more experience in the freelance writing industry, regularly reassess your skills, interests, and expertise.
    - Adjusting your niche and services over time can help you stay relevant and competitive in the evolving market.

Building your portfolio

Building a strong and diverse portfolio is crucial for showcasing your skills and attracting potential clients. This guide will provide you with essential tips and strategies for creating an impressive portfolio that highlights your writing abilities and expertise.

1. Identify your niche and target audience:
   - Determine your writing niche and the target audience you want to appeal to. This will help you tailor your portfolio to showcase your expertise and cater to the needs of your prospective clients.

2. Create a variety of writing samples:
   - Develop a diverse range of writing samples that demonstrate your versatility and skill in unique styles, formats, and topics. Include several types of content such as blog posts, articles, case studies, whitepapers, and social media content to showcase your range as a writer.

3. Focus on quality over quantity:
   - While it is important to have a diverse portfolio, prioritize quality over quantity.
   - Ensure that each writing sample showcases your best work and highlights your unique voice and style.

4. Include published work:
   - If you have previously published work, include these pieces in your portfolio as they demonstrate your credibility and professional experience.
   - Make sure to provide proper attribution and links to the original publications.

5. Write guest posts or contribute to blogs:
   - Offer to write guest posts for blogs or websites within your niche. This not only helps you build your portfolio but also expands your network and increases your online presence.

6. Create a personal blog or website:
   - Establish a personal blog or website where you can regularly publish your work, demonstrate your expertise, and build your online presence. This also provides a platform for your portfolio that is easy for clients to access and explore.

7. Optimize your portfolio for SEO:
   - Ensure that your online portfolio is optimized for search engines by including relevant keywords and phrases related to your niche and services. This can help increase your visibility and attract potential clients searching for freelance writers in your area of expertise.

8. Highlight your accomplishments and expertise:
   - Include a brief bio and list of accomplishments, such as awards, certifications, or notable clients with whom you have worked. This information can help establish your credibility and position you as an expert in your field.

9. Keep your portfolio updated:
   - Regularly update your portfolio with your latest and best work, removing outdated or less impressive pieces. Staying current helps demonstrate your ongoing commitment to excellence and professional growth.

10. Solicit client testimonials:
    - Ask satisfied clients to provide testimonials about your work and include them in your portfolio. Positive feedback from clients can help build trust and credibility with potential clients.

Creating an online presence

Having a professional online presence is crucial for attracting clients. creating a strong online presence is essential for promoting your services, showcasing your expertise, and attracting potential clients. This guide will provide you with essential tips and strategies for building and maintaining a professional online presence.

1. Develop a personal website or blog:
   - Create a personal website or blog to serve as your online hub, showcasing your portfolio, writing services, and expertise.
   - Choose a clean and professional design that is easy to navigate and reflects your personal brand.

2. Optimize your website for search engines:
   - Ensure that your website is optimized for search engines by including relevant keywords, phrases, and metadata related to your niche and services. This can help improve your search engine rankings and attract potential clients searching for freelance writers in your area of expertise.

3. Create and maintain social media profiles:
   - Establish and maintain profiles on popular social media platforms, such as LinkedIn, Twitter, and Facebook, to expand your online presence and connect with potential clients, peers, and industry influencers.

4. Share your work on social media:
   - Regularly share your published work, blog posts, and updates on your social media profiles to showcase your writing skills, engage with your audience, and increase your visibility.

5. Engage with your target audience:
   - Participate in online discussions, forums, and groups related to your niche and target audience. Engaging with your audience can help you establish yourself as an expert, build relationships, and attract potential clients.

6. Network with industry professionals:
   - Connect with other freelance writers, editors, and industry professionals on social media and professional networking platforms. Building relationships with industry peers can lead to new opportunities, collaborations, and valuable insights.

7. Guest post on relevant blogs and websites:
   - Offer to write guest posts for blogs or websites within your niche. Guest posting not only helps you build your portfolio but also expands your network and increases your online presence.

8. Create valuable and shareable content:
   - Regularly produce high-quality, engaging content that provides value to your target audience and is likely to be shared by others. Shareable content can help increase your visibility and attract potential clients.

9. Monitor your online reputation:
   - Regularly search for your name and monitor mentions of your work online to stay informed about your online reputation.
   - Address any negative feedback or comments professionally and promptly to maintain a positive image.

10. Update your online presence consistently:
    - Keep your website, portfolio, and social media profiles up to date with your latest work, accomplishments, and expertise.
    - Consistently maintaining your online presence can help you stay relevant and competitive in the freelance writing market.

Learning to pitch your services

Mastering the art of pitching your services is essential for attracting clients and securing writing projects. This guide will provide you with essential tips and strategies for crafting effective pitches that showcase your expertise and demonstrate the value of your writing services.

1. Identify your target clients:
   - Research and identify the types of clients you want to work with, such as businesses, publications, or individual clients within your niche.
   - Understanding your target clients can help you tailor your pitch to their specific needs and interests.

2. Develop a unique selling proposition (USP):
   - Create a unique selling proposition that sets you apart from other freelance writers and highlights your expertise, skills, and the value you bring to clients.
   - Your USP should be concise, compelling, and tailored to your target clients.

3. Craft a professional pitch template:
   - Develop a professional pitch template that can be customized for each client or project. Your pitch should include an introduction, a brief overview of your expertise, a description of your services, and a call to action.

4. Personalize your pitch:
   - Customize your pitch for each client or project by addressing the recipient by name, referencing their specific needs or challenges, and demonstrating how your services can provide a solution. Personalizing your pitch can help you establish a connection and stand out from other writers.

5. Keep your pitch concise and focused:
   - Ensure that your pitch is concise, focused, and easy to read by avoiding excessive jargon, lengthy sentences, and unnecessary information. Aim to convey the most essential information in a clear and engaging manner.

6. Showcase your relevant work samples:
   - Include links to relevant work samples or your portfolio within your pitch to demonstrate your writing skills and expertise. Select samples that align with the client's industry or the type of project for which you are pitching.

7. Follow submission guidelines:
   - When pitching to publications or websites, carefully read and follow their submission guidelines. This demonstrates your professionalism and attention to detail, increasing your chances of being considered for a project.

8. Be persistent and follow up:
   - If you have not received a response to your pitch after a reasonable amount of time, send a polite follow-up email to inquire about the status of your proposal. Persistence can pay off, and following up can help you stay top-of-mind for potential clients.

9. Learn from rejections and feedback:
   - Use rejections and feedback from clients to refine your pitching strategy and improve your skills. Analyse what worked and what did not in your previous pitches and apply those insights to future pitches.

10. Continuously improve your pitching skills:
   - Invest in your professional development by attending workshops, webinars, or courses on pitching and freelance writing.
   - Continuously refining your pitching skills can help you stay competitive and increase your chances of success.

Finding assignments on job boards and freelancing platforms

Finding assignments on job boards and freelancing platforms can provide a steady stream of work opportunities. This guide will provide you with essential tips and strategies for effectively using these resources to secure writing projects and build your freelance writing career.

1. Identify relevant job boards and platforms:
   - Research and compile a list of job boards and freelancing platforms that cater to freelance writers and your niche.
   - Some popular options include Upwork, Freelancer, Fiverr, ProBlogger Job Board, and Contena, but there may be others specific to your area of expertise.

2. Create professional profiles:
   - Set up comprehensive and professional profiles on your chosen platforms, including a well-written bio, a link to your portfolio, your expertise, and your rates. A polished profile can help you stand out to potential clients and increase your chances of being hired.

3. Customize your search:
   - Tailor your search on job boards and platforms to focus on opportunities that align with your niche, expertise, and desired rates. This can help you save time by narrowing down the list of potential assignments and increase your chances of securing relevant projects.

4. Set up job alerts:
   - Many job boards and platforms offer email alerts or notifications for new job postings that match your criteria. Set up alerts to receive updates about relevant opportunities, helping you stay informed and apply quickly.

5. Write tailored proposals:
   - When applying for assignments, customize your proposal to address the specific requirements and expectations outlined in the job posting.
   - Demonstrate how your skills and expertise make you the ideal candidate for the project.

6. Include relevant work samples:
   - Include links to relevant work samples or your portfolio when applying for assignments. Select samples that showcase your skills in the context of the project you are applying for.

7. Manage your workload:
   - Keep track of your current workload and the time required for each assignment when applying for new projects. Avoid overcommitting to ensure you can deliver high-quality work and meet deadlines.

8. Maintain a good reputation:
   - Deliver high-quality work, meet deadlines, and maintain professional communication with clients to build a powerful reputation on freelancing platforms.
   - Positive feedback and ratings can help you secure more assignments and attract higher-paying clients.

9. Network with other freelancers and clients:
   - Engage with other freelance writers and clients on freelancing platforms to build relationships and gain insights into industry trends and opportunities.
   - Networking can lead to referrals, collaborations, and new assignments.

10. Diversify your client sources:
    - While job boards and freelancing platforms can be a valuable source of assignments, do not rely solely on these resources.
    - Continuously seek out other avenues for finding work, such as networking, pitching directly to clients, or guest posting.

Networking with potential clients

Networking is essential for connecting with potential clients and expanding your professional opportunities. This guide will provide you with essential tips and strategies for building and maintaining a strong professional network to support your freelance writing career.

1. Leverage social media platforms:
   - Utilize social media platforms like LinkedIn, Twitter, and Facebook to connect with potential clients, other freelance writers, and industry influencers.
   - Share your work, engage in discussions, and showcase your expertise to increase your visibility and credibility.

2. Attend industry events and conferences:
   - Attend relevant events, conferences, and workshops in your niche, either in-person or virtually, to meet potential clients and expand your professional network.
   - Take advantage of networking opportunities during these events to introduce yourself and discuss your services.

3. Join online forums and communities:
   - Participate in online forums, groups, and communities related to your niche or the freelance writing industry.
   - Engage in discussions, provide valuable insights, and offer support to establish yourself as an expert and build relationships with potential clients.

4. Offer guest posts or collaborations:
   - Reach out to blogs, websites, or publications within your niche to offer guest posts or collaborate on projects. Guest posting and collaborations can help you expand your network, increase your visibility, and showcase your writing skills.

5. Create a professional email signature:
   - Include a professional email signature in your correspondence, featuring your name, contact information, website, and social media profiles. This can help potential clients easily find and connect with you.

6. Network with local businesses and organizations:
   - Connect with local businesses, organizations, and community groups in your niche or region. Introduce yourself, discuss your services, and explore potential opportunities for collaboration or freelance work.

7. Ask for referrals and recommendations:
   - Ask satisfied clients, colleagues, and peers for referrals or recommendations to expand your network and attract new clients. Positive word-of-mouth can be a powerful tool for growing your freelance writing business.

8. Attend networking events and meetups:
   - Join networking events, meetups, or co-working spaces tailored to freelancers, digital nomads, or professionals in your industry. These events can provide valuable opportunities to connect with potential clients and other professionals in your field.

9. Follow up with new contacts:
   - After meeting new contacts at events or online, follow up with a personalized email or message expressing your gratitude for the connection and reiterating your interest in working together.
   - Maintaining open communication can help you build strong relationships and stay top-of-mind for potential clients.

10. Continuously nurture your network:
   - Regularly engage with your professional network through social media, email, or in-person interactions.
   - Share updates about your work, offer support, and provide valuable insights to maintain relationships and demonstrate your expertise.

Setting your rates

Setting your rates is a crucial aspect of managing your business and ensuring your financial success. This guide will provide you with essential tips and strategies for determining and communicating your rates to potential clients.

1. Research industry rates:
   - Start by researching the standard rates for freelance writers in your niche and experience level.
   - Consult industry surveys, rate calculators, or freelance writing forums to gather information about the current market rates.

2. Consider your experience and expertise:
   - Evaluate your experience, skills, and expertise in your niche, and factor these into your rate determination.
   - If you have specialized knowledge or a unique skill set, you may be able to charge higher rates than a generalist writer.

3. Calculate your desired income:
   - Determine your desired annual income, considering your living expenses, taxes, and desired savings. Divide this figure by the number of billable hours you plan to work each year to calculate your target hourly rate.

4. Factor in your overhead costs:
   - Consider the costs associated with running your freelance writing business, such as internet access, software subscriptions, and travel expenses. Incorporate these overhead costs into your rate calculations to ensure you are covering your expenses.

5. Decide on a pricing structure:
   - Choose a pricing structure that works best for your services, such as hourly rates, per-word rates, or project-based fees. Each structure has its pros and cons, so consider the nature of your work and your clients' preferences when making your decision.

6. Create a rate sheet:
   - Develop a rate sheet that clearly outlines your pricing structure, rates, and any additional fees or discounts you may offer. A rate sheet can serve as a reference when discussing your fees with potential clients and help you maintain consistency in your pricing.

7. Be flexible and open to negotiation:
   - Recognize that some clients may have specific budget constraints or may request a lower rate in exchange for a long-term partnership or bulk work. Be open to negotiation while ensuring that your rates remain fair and sustainable for your business.

8. Communicate your value:
   - When discussing your rates with potential clients, emphasize the value you bring to their project, such as your expertise, experience, and the quality of your work. Demonstrating the benefits of working with you can help justify your rates and secure clients.

9. Regularly review and adjust your rates:
   - Periodically review your rates and adjust based on changes in the market, your experience level, and your financial goals. Regularly updating your rates can help you stay competitive and ensure you are fairly compensated for your work.

10. Stand your ground:
    - While it is important to be open to negotiation, do not undervalue your work or accept rates that are unsustainable for your business. Be confident in your rates and be prepared to walk away from potential clients who are unwilling to pay a fair price for your services.

Developing a system for managing projects and deadlines

Effective management of projects and deadlines is essential to maintaining your reputation, delivering high-quality work, and ensuring client satisfaction. This guide will provide you with essential tips and strategies for creating a system to manage your projects and deadlines.

1. Set clear expectations with clients:
   - At the beginning of each project, establish clear expectations with your clients regarding deliverables, deadlines, and communication preferences. This can help prevent misunderstandings and ensure both parties are on the same page.

2. Break projects into manageable tasks:
   - Divide each project into smaller, manageable tasks with specific milestones and deadlines. This can help you maintain focus and track your progress more efficiently.

3. Use a project management tool:
   - Leverage project management tools or applications, such as Trello, Asana, or Basecamp, to organise your tasks, deadlines, and communications. These tools can help you stay on top of your projects and collaborate effectively with clients and team members.

4. Prioritize your tasks:
   - Determine which tasks are most urgent or important and prioritize them in your schedule. This can help you stay focused on the most critical aspects of your projects and ensure you meet deadlines.

5. Develop a daily routine:
   - Establish a consistent daily routine that includes dedicated time for working on your projects, as well as breaks and self-care activities. A structured routine can help you maintain productivity and prevent burnout.

6. Set realistic deadlines:
   - When setting deadlines for your projects, factor in your workload, other commitments, and potential obstacles. Ensure that your deadlines are realistic and attainable to avoid unnecessary stress and maintain a healthy work-life balance.

7. Communicate proactively with clients:
   - Regularly update your clients on your progress and any challenges or delays you may encounter. Open and proactive communication can help build trust and maintain strong working relationships with your clients.

8. Monitor your progress:
   - Periodically review your progress on each project and adjust your schedule or workload as needed.
   - Monitoring your progress can help you identify potential issues early and ensure you stay on track to meet your deadlines.

9. Learn from your experiences:
   - Analyse your past projects and identify areas for improvement in your project management process.

- Continuously refine your system based on your experiences and lessons learned.

10. Maintain a healthy work-life balance:
    - While it is essential to manage your projects and deadlines effectively, do not neglect your personal well-being.
    - Take regular breaks, engage in hobbies, and maintain a healthy work-life balance to prevent burnout and ensure long-term success in your freelance writing career.

Improving your writing and research skills

Continuously honing your writing and research skills is essential to producing high-quality work and staying competitive in the market. This guide will provide you with essential tips and strategies for improving your writing and research skills as a freelance writer.

1. Read widely and critically:
   - Expose yourself to various writing styles, genres, and subjects to expand your knowledge and understanding of different writing techniques.
   - Reading critically can also help you identify strengths and weaknesses in your writing and inspire you to experiment with innovative approaches.

2. Take online courses and workshops:
   - Enrol in online writing and research courses, workshops, or webinars to learn new techniques, receive feedback, and stay current with industry trends.
   - Platforms like Coursera, Udemy, and MasterClass offer a variety of courses for writers of all levels.

3. Join writing groups and communities:
   - Connect with other freelance writers, digital nomads, or professionals in your niche by joining writing groups or online communities.
   - Sharing your work, discussing challenges, and offering feedback can help you improve your skills and expand your network.

4. Practice regularly:
   - Set aside dedicated time for writing practice, focusing on distinct aspects of your craft, such as storytelling, grammar, or style. Regular practice can help you refine your skills and develop a strong, unique writing voice.

5. Seek feedback and be open to criticism:
   - Share your work with peers, mentors, or professional editors to receive constructive feedback and suggestions for improvement. Embrace criticism as an opportunity to grow and develop your writing skills.

6. Keep a writing journal:
   - Maintain a writing journal to record your thoughts, ideas, and observations. Reflecting on your experiences can help you develop a richer understanding of your writing process and inspire current ideas for your projects.

7. Develop strong research skills:
   - Familiarize yourself with various research methods, such as online searches, interviews, or surveys, and practice applying these techniques to your writing projects. Developing strong research skills can help you produce well-informed, accurate, and engaging content.

8. Utilize writing and editing tools:
   - Leverage writing and editing tools, such as Grammarly, Hemingway Editor, or Scrivener, to help you refine your writing, identify errors, and maintain consistency in your work.

9. Stay up to date with industry news and trends:
   - Follow industry blogs, publications, and social media accounts to stay informed about the latest trends, best practices, and changes in the freelance writing market. Staying current can help you adapt your writing and research skills to meet the evolving needs of your clients.

10. Set personal development goals:
   - Identify areas for improvement in your writing and research skills and set specific, measurable goals for your personal development.
   - Regularly review your progress and adjust your goals as needed to ensure you continue to grow as a writer.

PROOFREADING

As a digital nomad, you are always on the lookout for flexible, location-independent work. Becoming an online proofreader can be a perfect fit! In this guide, we will explore what proofreaders do, the differences between proofreaders and copy editors, and how you can become a successful proofreader online.

Understand the role of a proofreader

As a digital nomad, building a successful proofreading business can offer flexibility and financial stability while traveling the world. This guide will cover the essential steps to become an efficient proofreader, ensuring the content you review is error-free and polished.

1. Develop your skills:
   - Improve your language and grammar skills by taking online courses, reading books, or using language learning apps like Grammarly or Hemingway.
   - Familiarize yourself with various style guides, such as the Chicago Manual of Style, Associated Press Stylebook, or the Modern Language Association (MLA) Handbook.
   - Practice proofreading by working on sample texts, freelance projects, or volunteering for non-profit organizations.

2. Create an online presence:
   - Build a professional website showcasing your services, portfolio, and client testimonials.
   - Develop a LinkedIn profile highlighting your proofreading skills.
   - Join online forums, social media groups, and communities related to proofreading and writing.

3. Invest in necessary tools and resources:
   - Acquire a reliable laptop with a good internet connection.
   - Utilize proofreading software, such as Grammarly, ProWritingAid, or Microsoft Word.
   - Create a comfortable and organized workspace, including an ergonomic chair and noise-cancelling headphones.

4. Find work opportunities:
   - Browse job boards and freelancing platforms like Upwork, Freelancer, or FlexJobs.
   - Reach out to potential clients directly through social media, email, or online networking events.
   - Develop relationships with content creators, publishers, and other professionals in need of proofreading services.

5. Set competitive rates:
   - Research industry standards and competitor rates to determine your pricing.
   - Consider factors such as the complexity of the project, turnaround time, and your level of expertise.

- Offer a range of pricing options, such as hourly rates, per-word rates, or project-based fees.

6. Communicate effectively with clients:
   - Maintain clear and professional communication throughout the project.
   - Provide a detailed explanation of your services, turnaround time, and pricing.
   - Be responsive and open to feedback or questions from clients.

7. Continuously improve your skills:
   - Stay updated on industry trends, tools, and best practices.
   - Attend webinars, workshops, and industry events to network with professionals and learn new techniques.
   - Pursue professional certifications or training programs, such as the courses offered by the Editorial Freelancers Association (EFA) or the Society for Editors and Proofreaders (SfEP).

8. Manage your time and workload:
   - Use project management tools like Trello or Asana to track tasks, deadlines, and client information.
   - Prioritize projects based on urgency and importance.
   - Establish a consistent work routine and set boundaries to maintain a healthy work-life balance.

Know the requirements for becoming an online proofreader

While a degree may not be mandatory, specific skills and qualities are essential for success in this field. This guide will outline the key requirements for becoming an online proofreader.

1. Develop strong language skills:
   - Master English grammar, spelling, punctuation, and syntax.
   - Enhance your vocabulary and stay up to date with language changes and trends.
   - Consider learning a second language to broaden your client base.

2. Cultivate attention to detail:
   - Be meticulous and patient when reviewing texts.
   - Develop the ability to spot even the smallest errors.
   - Practice proofreading on a variety of content types, including blog posts, essays, and books.

3. Improve time management skills:
   - Learn to prioritize tasks and set deadlines.
   - Allocate sufficient time for each proofreading project, considering its length and complexity.
   - Use time management tools and techniques, such as the Pomodoro Technique or time blocking.

4. Familiarize yourself with style guides:
   - Study commonly used style guides like the Chicago Manual of Style, Associated Press Stylebook, or Modern Language Association (MLA) Handbook.

- Understand the differences between each style guide and when to apply them.
- Stay current with updates and changes to style guides.

5. Pursue relevant education and training:
   - Although not required, obtaining a degree in English, journalism, or a related field can enhance your credibility.
   - Enrol in proofreading courses, workshops, or certification programs to expand your skillset.
   - Join professional organizations, such as the Editorial Freelancers Association (EFA) or the Society for Editors and Proofreaders (SfEP), to access resources and networking opportunities.

6. Build your portfolio and gain experience:
   - Offer your services to friends, family, or local businesses to gain initial experience and build your portfolio.
   - Volunteer for non-profit organizations, schools, or online publications.
   - Pursue freelance proofreading projects on platforms like Upwork, Freelancer, or FlexJobs.

7. Market yourself effectively:
   - Create a professional website showcasing your services, portfolio, and client testimonials.
   - Develop a strong online presence through social media and networking platforms like LinkedIn.
   - Network with other professionals in the industry and join online communities related to proofreading and writing.

Follow these five steps to become an online proofreader

By following these five steps, you can establish yourself as an online proofreader, attract clients, and create a sustainable income source.

1. Take a proofreading course:
   - Enrol in an online proofreading course to improve your English skills and learn essential proofreading techniques.
   - Look for reputable providers offering comprehensive courses, such as Proofread Anywhere or The Writer's Workshop.
   - Complete the course and obtain a certification to add credibility to your resume.

2. Invest in the right software and tools:
   - Equip yourself with a laptop or desktop, a mouse, and essential software such as Microsoft Office, Google Docs, and Adobe Acrobat.
   - Consider using proofreading tools like Grammarly, ProWritingAid, or LanguageTool to enhance your accuracy and efficiency.
   - Familiarize yourself with different file formats and editing platforms commonly used in the industry.

3. Choose your proofreading niche:
   - Focus on specific proofreading services, such as academic, business, print media, or translation proofreading, depending on your interests and expertise.
   - Determine which niche aligns with your skills, background, and desired income potential.
   - Consider specializing further within a niche to differentiate yourself from competitors, such as focusing on proofreading medical research articles or legal documents.

4. Create a resume:
   - Highlight your relevant skills, experiences, and any proofreading courses you have taken.
   - Include any previous proofreading experience, even if it is informal, such as proofreading for classmates, co-workers, or friends.
   - Mention any additional skills, such as fluency in another language or expertise in a specific industry, which may appeal to potential clients.

5. Build your online presence:
   - Create a website or online portfolio showcasing your skills and services.
   - Include samples of your proofreading work, client testimonials, and your resume on your website.
   - Utilize social media platforms, such as LinkedIn, Twitter, and Facebook, to network with potential clients and other professionals in the industry.
   - Sign up for freelancing websites like Upwork, Freelancer, or Fiverr to promote your services and find clients.

Network and market your services

Networking and professional development are crucial components of building a successful online proofreading career as a digital nomad. By connecting with other proofreaders, editors, and writers, you can learn from their experiences, share best practices, and expand your professional network, increasing your chances of success in the industry.

1. Online forums and communities:
   - Join online forums and communities dedicated to proofreading, editing, and writing.
   - Engage in discussions, ask questions, and share your experiences with fellow professionals.
   - Some popular forums and communities include Absolute Write, the Editorial Freelancers Association, and the Society for Editors and Proofreaders.

2. Social media groups:
   - Utilize social media platforms such as Facebook, LinkedIn, and Twitter to connect with like-minded professionals.
   - Join groups and follow pages related to proofreading, editing, and writing.
   - Participate in group discussions, share relevant content, and network with other members.

3. Professional organizations:
   - Become a member of professional organizations for proofreaders and editors, such as the American Copy Editors Society (ACES) or the Chartered Institute of Editing and Proofreading (CIEP).

- These organizations often provide resources, job listings, and networking opportunities for their members.
- Attend meetings, workshops, and conferences organized by these associations to meet industry professionals and stay up to date on industry trends.

4. Industry events, webinars, and workshops:
   - Attend industry-specific events, webinars, and workshops to expand your knowledge and skills in proofreading, editing, and writing.
   - Many of these events can be attended virtually, allowing digital nomads to participate from anywhere in the world.
   - Use these events as opportunities to network with other professionals, learn about potential job openings, and discover new tools and techniques to improve your proofreading skills.

5. Build and maintain relationships:
   - Networking is an ongoing process, so make sure to maintain relationships with the contacts you make.
   - Reach out to your connections periodically, share relevant information or opportunities, and offer help when appropriate.
   - Cultivate relationships with both peers and potential clients to increase your chances of receiving referrals and securing new projects.

Keep learning and improving

It is essential to stay updated on industry trends and best practices. Continuously improving your skills and knowledge will not only enhance your services but also make you more competitive in the industry. Here is a guide to help you stay informed and grow as an online proofreader while exploring the world.

1. Read relevant blogs, articles, and books:
   - Follow industry-specific blogs and websites to stay updated on proofreading trends, techniques, and tools.
   - Subscribe to newsletters, read articles, and study books related to proofreading, editing, and writing.
   - Some popular resources include Copyediting.com, ProBlogger, and the books "The Copyeditor's Handbook" by Amy Einsohn and "The Elements of Style" by William Strunk Jr. and E.B. White.

2. Take advanced courses and certifications:
   - Pursue advanced courses and certifications in proofreading, editing, or writing to deepen your expertise and add credibility to your professional profile.
   - Look for courses and certifications from reputable organizations and institutions, such as the Poynter ACES Certificate in Editing, the University of Chicago's Editing Certificate, or specialized courses on platforms like Coursera, Udemy, or LinkedIn Learning.

3. Attend webinars and workshops:
   - Participate in webinars and workshops to learn from industry experts and improve your proofreading skills.
   - These events can cover assorted topics, such as mastering specific style guides, improving your editing efficiency, or learning about new tools and technologies in the industry.

- Many webinars and workshops are available online, making them accessible to digital nomads around the world.

4. Join industry-specific groups and forums:
   - As mentioned in the previous guide, engaging in online groups and forums related to proofreading, editing, and writing can help you stay informed about industry trends and best practices.
   - Use these platforms to ask questions, share your knowledge, and learn from fellow professionals.

5. Seek feedback and learn from your experiences:
   - Request feedback from your clients to identify areas where you can improve your proofreading skills.
   - Analyse your past work and learn from any mistakes or challenges you faced, applying those lessons to future projects.

Take a Proofreading Course

It is essential to invest in your skills and knowledge. Enrolling in a proofreading course can be a fantastic way to sharpen your abilities, learn the ins and outs of the profession, and potentially secure work with reputable companies. In this guide, we'll explore the benefits of enrolling in a proofreading course, like the one offered by Knowadays, and how it can help you succeed as a digital nomad proofreader.

1. Sharpen your skills:
   - A proofreading course will teach you essential techniques, such as grammar, punctuation, spelling, and formatting.
   - You will also learn how to spot common errors and inconsistencies, as well as how to apply various style guides in your work.
   - By completing a proofreading course, you will be more confident in your abilities and better equipped to provide high-quality services to your clients.

2. Learn the ins and outs of the profession:
   - A comprehensive proofreading course will also cover the business side of the industry, such as finding clients, setting rates, and managing projects.
   - You will gain insights into marketing your services, building a portfolio, and creating a professional online presence.
   - Understanding the practical aspects of the proofreading business will help you navigate the freelance landscape and succeed as a digital nomad.

3. Secure work with reputable companies:
   - Some proofreading courses, like the one offered by Knowadays, guarantee work with their partner companies upon completion.
   - This partnership can be an excellent opportunity to jumpstart your career, as you will have the chance to work with a reputable company like Proofed, gaining experience and building your portfolio.
   - Having a well-known company on your resume can also help you attract more clients and boost your credibility in the industry.

4. Network with fellow proofreaders:
   - Participating in a proofreading course can connect you with other professionals in the field.
   - Networking with your peers can lead to valuable relationships, potential collaborations, and a supportive community of like-minded individuals.
   - You may also learn about job opportunities, industry events, and other resources through your network.

5. Stay competitive in the market:
   - As a digital nomad proof-reader, it is crucial to stay competitive in the market.
   - Completing a proofreading course demonstrates your commitment to your craft and professionalism, setting you apart from others in the industry.
   - Clients will be more likely to choose a proofreader with formal training and a proven track record of success.

Use Freelance Job Platforms

It is essential to know where to find freelance job opportunities. Platforms like FlexJobs, Upwork, and Fiverr can provide numerous proofreading gigs to help you grow your client base and establish your reputation. In this guide, we will discuss the benefits of each platform and share a special promo code for FlexJobs to help you get started.

1. FlexJobs:
   - FlexJobs is a user-friendly platform dedicated to remote and flexible job opportunities, including proofreading.
   - It offers curated job listings, ensuring that you only see high-quality, legitimate job postings.
   - While FlexJobs requires a monthly subscription, you can use promo code NOMAD to receive a 30% discount on membership fees.
   - The platform has less competition than Upwork, making it easier to land gigs and build your client base.

2. Upwork:
   - Upwork is a popular freelance platform with a wide range of proofreading job opportunities.
   - It allows you to create a comprehensive profile, showcasing your skills, experience, and portfolio.
   - Although Upwork can be competitive, it offers a broad client base, giving you the chance to work on diverse projects and gain experience.
   - Upwork takes a percentage of your earnings as a service fee, but it decreases as you earn more with a specific client.

3. Fiverr:
   - Fiverr is a freelance platform where you can create service offerings, or "gigs," to attract clients looking for proofreading services.
   - This platform enables you to set your rates and define your proofreading packages, making it easy for clients to see what you offer.
   - Fiverr can be a great option for new proofreaders looking to build their portfolio and gain experience.

- Like Upwork, Fiverr takes a percentage of your earnings as a service fee.

Apply to Proofreading Companies

Applying to established proofreading companies like Scribendi and Scribbr can provide digital nomads with a stable source of income and flexible work arrangements. Although these companies have rigorous application processes, being accepted can lead to regular, well-paying assignments. In this guide, we will discuss the benefits of working with Scribendi and Scribbr and share tips for a successful application.

1. Scribendi:
   - Scribendi is a well-established proofreading and editing company that hires remote proofreaders and editors.
   - The company offers a variety of projects, from academic papers to business documents, allowing you to work on diverse assignments.
   - Scribendi has strict application requirements, including a university degree, native-level English proficiency, and at least three years of editing experience.
   - If accepted, you can expect regular assignments, fair compensation, and the flexibility to work from anywhere.

2. Scribbr:
   - Scribbr is another reputable proofreading and editing company that focuses primarily on academic documents.
   - The company hires remote proofreaders with a strong command of the English language and a background in academia.
   - Scribbr's application process includes a language quiz, an editing sample, and a comprehensive training program.
   - If accepted, you can enjoy a steady stream of work, competitive pay, and the freedom to work from any location.

Tips for a successful application: a. Review the company's requirements: Ensure you meet the eligibility criteria before applying and address these requirements in your application. b. Showcase your skills and experience: Highlight your relevant experience, qualifications, and skills that make you a suitable candidate for the role. c. Tailor your application: Customize your application to the specific company, demonstrating your familiarity with their services and target audience. d. Proofread your application: Make sure your application is error-free and well-written, as this reflects your proofreading abilities.

Network with Professional Proofreaders

Networking is a crucial component of building a successful online proofreading career as a digital nomad. Connecting with experienced proofreaders can lead to job referrals, valuable advice, and a support system that can help you navigate the industry. In this guide, we will discuss several ways to connect with professional proofreaders and maximize the benefits of networking.

1. Online forums and discussion boards:
   - Join online forums and discussion boards dedicated to proofreading, editing, and writing. These platforms can be a treasure trove of information and connections.

- Engage in discussions, ask questions, and share your experiences to build relationships with fellow proofreaders.
- Examples of such forums include Proz, Absolute Write, and the Editorial Freelancers Association forums.

2. Social media platforms:
   - Utilize social media platforms like LinkedIn, Facebook, and Twitter to connect with professional proofreaders and industry influencers.
   - Join proofreading and editing groups on Facebook and LinkedIn to engage in conversations, share resources, and learn from others in the industry.
   - Follow experienced proofreaders on Twitter and engage with their content to build a rapport.

3. Networking events and conferences:
   - Attend industry events, conferences, and workshops to meet and learn from other professionals in the field.
   - Participate in virtual events if you are unable to attend in-person gatherings due to your nomadic lifestyle.
   - Examples of events include the annual conferences of the Editorial Freelancers Association, the American Copy Editors Society, and the Society for Editors and Proofreaders.

4. Collaboration and mentorship:
   - Reach out to experienced proofreaders for mentorship or collaboration opportunities. Many professionals are happy to share their knowledge and expertise with those new to the industry.
   - Offer to assist with projects or work on a trial basis to demonstrate your skills and build trust with potential mentors or collaborators.

Keep Building Your Experience and Skills

As a digital nomad pursuing a successful online proofreading career, continuous skill development and leveraging your experience can help you secure higher-paying clients. In this guide, we will discuss strategies to increase your earnings as you gain experience in the field.

1. Invest in ongoing education:
   - Take advanced courses, attend webinars, and participate in workshops to further develop your proofreading skills.
   - Stay updated on industry trends, style guides, and best practices by reading relevant blogs, articles, and books.
   - Obtain certifications from reputable organizations, such as the Editorial Freelancers Association or the Society for Editors and Proofreaders, to showcase your expertise.

2. Leverage your niche expertise:
   - Specialize in a niche or industry that aligns with your interests and background, such as academic, legal, medical, or technical proofreading.
   - Use your specialized knowledge to target high-paying clients and secure premium rates for your services.

3. Showcase your experience and achievements:
   - Update your online portfolio and resume regularly to reflect your growing experience and skillset.
   - Highlight successful projects, testimonials from satisfied clients, and any awards or recognitions you have received in the industry.

4. Raise your rates strategically:
   - Review your rates periodically to ensure they align with your skills, experience, and the market value of your services.
   - Communicate rate increases to your clients with professionalism and confidence, emphasizing the value you bring to their projects.

5. Cultivate long-term client relationships:
   - Deliver high-quality work consistently to build trust and credibility with your clients.
   - Maintain open communication and be responsive to client feedback and concerns.
   - Offer additional services, such as editing or content creation, to existing clients for increased revenue opportunities.

6. Network and diversify your client base:
   - Connect with other proofreaders, editors, and writers through online forums, social media groups, and professional organizations.
   - Expand your client base by exploring new platforms, such as job boards, freelancing websites, or direct outreach to potential clients.

HOUSE & PET SITTING

International house and pet sitting offers a unique opportunity to travel the world while providing a valuable service to homeowners. This comprehensive guide will help you navigate the steps to become a successful international house and/or pet sitter.

Assessing your skills and suitability

It is essential to assess your skills and suitability for the role. This guide will help you evaluate your abilities and determine whether house or pet sitting is the right fit for your lifestyle and goals.

1. Self-Reflection:
   - Begin by asking yourself why you are interested in house or pet sitting.
   - Are you looking for a way to save money on accommodations, explore new locations, or gain experience working with animals?
   - Identifying your motivations can help you decide if house or pet sitting aligns with your goals and lifestyle.

2. Experience with animals:
   - If you are considering pet sitting, evaluate your experience and comfort level with animals.
   - Have you owned pets in the past or spent time caring for others' pets?
   - Are you knowledgeable about the specific needs and behaviours of the pets you will be sitting? Being comfortable and experienced with animals is essential for a successful pet sitting experience.

3. Responsibility and reliability:
   - House and pet sitting require a prominent level of responsibility and reliability.
   - Consider whether you can commit to the required time frame, provide consistent care for the home and pets, and be responsive to the homeowner's needs and concerns.

4. Adaptability and flexibility:
   - As a house or pet sitter, you will need to adapt to different living situations, routines, and pet personalities.
   - Assess your ability to be flexible and adapt to new environments and challenges while maintaining your work and personal responsibilities.

5. Organizational and time management skills:
   - Managing your work as a digital nomad while fulfilling your duties as a house or pet sitter requires strong organizational and time management skills.
   - Reflect on your ability to balance multiple responsibilities, prioritize tasks, and maintain a schedule.

6. Communication skills:
   - Effective communication is crucial when working with homeowners and addressing any issues that arise during the house or pet sitting assignment.
   - Assess your communication skills, both in-person and through digital channels, to ensure you can effectively convey information and respond to concerns.

7. Problem-solving skills:
   - Unexpected issues can arise during house or pet sitting assignments, such as maintenance problems or pet health concerns.
   - Consider your ability to think critically, problem-solve, and address challenges as they occur.

8. Personal background and references:
   - Homeowners may require background checks, references, or proof of identity before entrusting their home and pets to you.

- Reflect on your personal background, professional experience, and character references to ensure you can meet these requirements.

9. Research and knowledge:
   - Familiarise yourself with the responsibilities and expectations of house and pet sitting, including legal and insurance considerations.
   - Understanding the ins and outs of house and pet sitting can help you make an informed decision about your suitability for the role.

10. Assess the fit with your digital nomad lifestyle:
    - Finally, consider how house and pet sitting aligns with your digital nomad lifestyle and work commitments.
    - Ensure that you can balance the demands of your work while providing quality care for the home and pets in your charge.

Gaining experience and references

Gaining experience and obtaining references are crucial steps in building trust with potential clients. This guide will provide you with tips and strategies for gaining relevant experience and securing valuable references as a house or pet sitter.

1. Start with friends and family:
   - Begin by offering your house or pet sitting services to friends and family. This allows you to gain experience and build your reputation in a familiar and comfortable environment.
   - Once you have successfully completed a few assignments, ask your friends or family members to provide you with written references or testimonials.

2. Volunteer at local animal shelters or organizations:
   - If you are interested in pet sitting, volunteering at local animal shelters or rescue organizations can help you gain hands-on experience with animals, learn about their care and behaviour, and demonstrate your commitment to animal welfare.
   - Be sure to ask for a reference letter or certificate of completion from the organization once your volunteer term has ended.

3. Create a professional profile on house or pet sitting platforms:
   - Sign up for reputable house or pet sitting platforms, such as TrustedHousesitters, HouseCarers, or Nomador, and create a professional profile.
   - Showcase your skills, experience, and any relevant certifications, and ask for endorsements from previous clients or friends who can vouch for your abilities.

4. Offer your services in local online groups or forums:
   - Join local online groups, forums, or community pages dedicated to house or pet sitting and offer your services.
   - Start by charging a lower rate or offering your services for free in exchange for a reference. As you gain more experience and positive reviews, you can gradually increase your rates.

5. Network with other house or pet sitters:
   - Connect with other house or pet sitters in your area or within the digital nomad community. Networking can help you learn from others' experiences, share tips, and potentially receive referrals from sitters who have more assignments than they can handle.

6. Complete relevant training or certifications:
   - Consider completing relevant training or certifications to improve your skills and credibility as a house or pet sitter. Courses in pet first aid, animal behaviour, or home maintenance can provide you with valuable knowledge and demonstrate your commitment to the role.

7. Document your experiences:
   - Create a portfolio or blog documenting your house or pet sitting experiences, including photos, stories, and any challenges you have overcome. This can serve as a powerful tool for showcasing your skills and attracting potential clients.

8. Build your social media presence:
   - Leverage your social media accounts to share your house or pet sitting experiences, showcase your skills, and connect with potential clients.
   - Make sure your profiles are professional and consistent across platforms.

9. Be proactive in seeking references:
   - After completing a successful house or pet sitting assignment, always ask the homeowner for a reference or review. The more positive references you have, the more attractive you will be to potential clients.

10. Provide excellent service:
   - The best way to gain experience and references is to provide exceptional service. Be responsible, reliable, and attentive to the needs of the homeowners and pets in your care. A formidable reputation for excellent service will lead to more opportunities and positive references.

Obtaining necessary certifications

Obtaining relevant certifications can help digital nomads build their credibility as house or pet sitters and set them apart from the competition. This guide will provide information on the types of certifications that can benefit house and pet sitters, as well as tips on how to obtain them.

1. Pet First Aid and CPR Certification:
   - A Pet First Aid and CPR Certification can be invaluable for pet sitters, as it equips them with the skills to handle medical emergencies involving pets.
   - Several organizations, such as the American Red Cross, PetTech, or ProTrainings, offer pet first aid and CPR courses, both online and in-person.

2. Animal Behaviour and Training Certifications:
   - Understanding animal behaviour and training techniques can be beneficial for pet sitters looking to provide exceptional care.
   - Consider obtaining certifications from organizations like the Certification Council for Professional Dog Trainers (CCPDT) or the International Association of Animal Behaviour Consultants (IAABC).

3. Basic Home Maintenance Certification:
   - A basic home maintenance certification can be useful for house sitters, as it demonstrates their ability to handle minor repairs and maintenance tasks.

- Local community colleges or vocational schools may offer courses in basic home repair or maintenance, covering topics such as plumbing, electrical systems, and general household repairs.

4. Background Check Certification:
   - Some house or pet sitting platforms require sitters to obtain a background check certification.
   - Websites like Sterling Volunteers, Checkr, or First Advantage offer background check services tailored to the needs of house and pet sitters, which can help establish trust with potential clients.

5. Online House or Pet Sitting Courses:
   - Several online platforms offer courses specifically designed for house or pet sitters, covering topics such as pet care, house sitting etiquette, and managing a house or pet sitting business.
   - Websites like Udemy, Coursera, or even house and pet sitting platforms like TrustedHousesitters offer courses that can help you gain knowledge and earn a certificate upon completion.

6. Insurance and Bonding:
   - While not a certification per se, obtaining insurance and bonding can provide added security for both you and the homeowner.
   - Look for insurance providers that specialize in house or pet sitting, such as Pet Sitters Associates and consider obtaining a surety bond as an added layer of protection.

7. Language Certifications:
   - If you plan to house or pet sit internationally, having language certifications can be an asset. Proficiency in the local language can facilitate communication with homeowners and help you navigate the local community.
   - Language certifications, such as the TOEFL, IELTS, or DELE, can demonstrate your language skills to potential clients.

Creating an online presence

Creating a strong online presence is crucial for digital nomads seeking to become successful house or pet sitters. By following the tips and strategies outlined in this guide, you can effectively showcase your skills, experience, and professionalism, attract potential clients, and build a thriving house or pet sitting business as a digital nomad.

1. Build a professional website:
   - A well-designed website serves as a digital resume, showcasing your services, experience, and testimonials from previous clients.
   - Use website builders like Wix, Squarespace, or WordPress to create a visually appealing, easy-to-navigate site that highlights your house or pet sitting skills and achievements.

2. Create a blog:
   - A blog can help you share your experiences, expertise, and stories as a house or pet sitter. Consistently posting engaging content not only demonstrates your commitment to the profession but can also improve your website's search engine rankings, making it more visible to potential clients.

- Join house and pet sitting platforms: Sign up for reputable house and pet sitting platforms like TrustedHousesitters, HouseCarers, or Nomador. Create detailed, well-written profiles that showcase your experience, skills, and any relevant certifications. Be sure to include high-quality photos and request endorsements from previous clients or friends who can vouch for your abilities.

3. Optimize your website for SEO:
   - Optimizing your website for search engines can help improve its visibility and attract more potential clients.
   - Research relevant keywords related to house or pet sitting and incorporate them into your website's content, meta tags, and headings. Additionally, regularly update your site with fresh content and ensure it is mobile-friendly.

4. Leverage social media:
   - Create professional social media profiles on platforms like Facebook, Instagram, LinkedIn, and Twitter.
   - Share your house or pet sitting experiences, showcase your skills, and engage with potential clients. Make sure your profiles are consistent across platforms and regularly updated with relevant content.

5. Participate in online forums and communities:
   - Join online forums, communities, or social media groups related to house or pet sitting, digital nomadism, or local community pages.
   - Engage with members, share your expertise, and offer your services to build your reputation and attract potential clients.

6. Collect and showcase testimonials:
   - Gather testimonials from satisfied clients and feature them prominently on your website, social media profiles, and house or pet sitting platform profiles.
   - Positive reviews and testimonials can help build trust with potential clients and demonstrate your commitment to providing excellent service.

7. Develop a personal brand:
   - Develop a personal brand that reflects your unique skills, values, and expertise as a house or pet sitter.
   - Use a consistent colour scheme, font, and tone of voice across all online platforms, and ensure your branding is present in your website, social media profiles, and email communications.

8. Network with other professionals:
   - Connect with other house or pet sitters, digital nomads, and industry professionals. Networking can lead to collaborations, referrals, and valuable insights to help you grow your business and improve your online presence.

9. Monitor and update your online presence:
   - Regularly monitor your online presence to ensure all information is up-to-date, accurate, and consistent across platforms.
   - Respond to comments, messages, and reviews promptly and professionally.

Signing up for house and pet sitting platforms

Signing up for house and pet sitting platforms is a crucial step for digital nomads looking to become successful in this field. By following the steps outlined in this guide, you can create a compelling profile that showcases your skills, experience, and professionalism, helping you attract potential clients and secure house or pet sitting assignments as a digital nomad.

Create a profile on these platforms, highlighting your experience and qualifications, and start applying for suitable assignments.

These platforms provide a convenient marketplace for sitters to showcase their skills and experience, while homeowners can easily browse and choose the right sitter for their needs. This guide will help you understand how to sign up for house and pet sitting platforms and create a profile that stands out.

1. Research and select the right platform(s):
   - Before signing up, research various house and pet sitting platforms to determine which ones align best with your needs, target market, and preferences.
   - Some popular platforms include TrustedHousesitters, HouseCarers, Nomador, and MindMyHouse. Consider factors such as platform fees, geographic reach, and the type of services offered.

2. Create an account:
   - Once you have chosen a platform, create an account using a professional email address.
   - Some platforms may require you to sign up as a homeowner or a sitter or both. Be sure to sign up for the correct account type based on your objectives.

3. Fill out your profile information:
   - Complete your profile with accurate and detailed information about yourself, your house or pet sitting experience, and your skills.
   - Be honest and authentic in your description, focusing on your strengths and what sets you apart from other sitters.

4. Upload high-quality photos:
   - Include high-quality photos in your profile that showcase your personality and experience.
   - Include a clear and friendly profile picture, images of you with pets, and photos from previous house or pet sitting assignments if available.
   - Make sure the photos are well-lit and visually appealing.

5. Add relevant certifications and qualifications:
   - List any relevant certifications or qualifications, such as pet first aid, animal behaviour training, or home maintenance, which can help you stand out as a professional and competent sitter.
   - Be prepared to provide proof of these certifications if requested by homeowners.

6. Provide a list of services:
   - Clearly outline the services you offer as a house or pet sitter. This can include pet care (e.g., walking, feeding, administering medication), home maintenance, plant care, and any additional services you are willing to provide.

7. Set your availability and preferred locations:
   - Update your availability calendar to reflect when you are open to house or pet sitting assignments.
   - Indicate your preferred locations, such as specific countries, regions, or cities, to help homeowners find you based on their needs.

8. Obtain and showcase endorsements and testimonials:
   - Request endorsements or testimonials from friends, family, or previous clients who can vouch for your house or pet sitting skills. These endorsements can help build trust and credibility with potential clients.

9. Apply for assignments:
   - Once your profile is complete, start browsing and applying for house or pet sitting assignments that match your skills, interests, and availability.
   - Tailor your application to each homeowner's needs, highlighting your relevant experience and qualifications.

10. Stay active and engaged on the platform:
    - Regularly update your profile, availability, and preferences to ensure your information is current and accurate.
    - Respond promptly to messages from homeowners and actively participate in the platform's community, if available.

Craft a compelling application

Crafting a compelling house or pet sitting application is crucial for digital nomads looking to stand out from the competition and secure assignments. By following the tips and strategies outlined in this guide, you can create an engaging and persuasive application that showcases your skills, experience, and commitment to providing excellent service as a house or pet sitter.

1. Research the homeowner's needs and preferences:
   - Before crafting your application, take the time to thoroughly read the homeowner's listing and understand their specific needs and preferences. This will help you tailor your application to their requirements and demonstrate your attention to detail.

2. Address the homeowner by name:
   - If possible, address the homeowner by their name in your application. This adds an individualized touch and shows that you have taken the time to read their listing carefully.

3. Introduce yourself and your experience:
   - Begin your application with a brief introduction that highlights your experience as a house or pet sitter.
   - Mention any relevant qualifications or certifications you hold, as well as the number of assignments you have completed or the duration of your experience in the field.

4. Explain why you are a good fit for the assignment:
   - Outline the specific skills and attributes that make you a suitable candidate for the assignment. For example, if the homeowner requires a sitter with experience caring for elderly pets, mention any relevant experience or training you have in this area.

5. Provide examples of previous assignments:
   - Include examples of previous house or pet sitting assignments you have completed, along with any positive feedback or testimonials from homeowners. This can help to build trust and showcase your track record of providing excellent service.

6. Emphasize your adaptability and problem-solving abilities:
   - As a digital nomad, you are likely to encounter various challenges while house or pet sitting.
   - Emphasize your adaptability, resourcefulness, and problem-solving abilities in your application, providing examples of situations where you have successfully navigated unexpected challenges.

7. Mention your love for animals and/or travel:
   - If you are passionate about animals, travel, or both, share this enthusiasm in your application. This can help to demonstrate your genuine interest in house or pet sitting and create a connection with the homeowner.

8. Offer to provide additional information or references:
   - At the end of your application, offer to provide any additional information or references the homeowner may require. This shows your willingness to be transparent and can help to build trust.

9. Proofread your application:
   - Before submitting your application, proofread it carefully for any spelling, grammar, or punctuation errors. A well-written, error-free application reflects your professionalism and attention to detail.

10. Keep it concise and focused:
    - While it is essential to provide enough information to showcase your skills and experience, avoid making your application too long or overly detailed. Aim to keep it concise and focused, ensuring that every sentence is relevant and adds value to your application.

Prepare for interviews and background checks

As a digital nomad seeking house or pet sitting assignments, you may be required to participate in interviews and background checks. These processes help homeowners assess your suitability for the assignment and ensure the safety and security of their homes and pets. This guide will provide tips on how to prepare for interviews and background checks to increase your chances of being selected for house or pet sitting assignments.

1. Review your profile and application:
   - Before an interview, review your profile and the application you submitted to the homeowner.
   - Make sure you are familiar with the information you provided and are prepared to answer any questions or provide further details about your experience and qualifications.

2. Research the homeowner and their needs:
   - Read the homeowner's listing carefully and take note of any specific requirements or preferences they mentioned. This will help you tailor your interview responses to their needs and demonstrate your attention to detail.

3. Prepare answers to common interview questions:
   - Anticipate common interview questions, such as:
   - Why are you interested in this house or pet sitting assignment?
   - Can you provide examples of your previous house or pet sitting experiences?
   - How do you handle emergencies or unexpected situations?
   - What are your strategies for managing multiple responsibilities, such as pet care and home maintenance?

Practice your answers to ensure you can respond confidently and concisely during the interview.

4. Prepare questions to ask the homeowner:
   - Prepare a list of questions to ask the homeowner about their home, pets, and any specific requirements they have for the assignment. This will help you gain a better understanding of their expectations and demonstrate your interest in the position.

5. Dress professionally and maintain a clean background for video interviews:
   - If your interview is conducted via video call, dress professionally and ensure your background is clean and free from distractions. This will help you make a good impression and convey a sense of professionalism.

6. Be honest and transparent:
   - During the interview, be honest and transparent about your skills, experience, and any potential limitations you may have. Homeowners appreciate honesty and are more likely to trust a candidate who is upfront about their abilities.

7. Obtain necessary documents for background checks:
   - If a homeowner requests a background check, be prepared to provide any necessary documentation, such as your ID or proof of address.
   - Some platforms may offer background checks as part of their services, but you may also need to provide these documents independently.

8. Address any concerns or discrepancies in your background check:
   - If there are any concerns or discrepancies in your background check, be prepared to address them and provide any necessary explanations or documentation. This can help to alleviate any concerns the homeowner may have and demonstrate your commitment to transparency.

9. Follow up after the interview:
   - After the interview, send a follow-up email to thank the homeowner for their time and reiterate your interest in the assignment. This can help to reinforce your professionalism and leave a positive impression on the homeowner.

Understand the expectations and responsibilities

Becoming a successful house or pet sitter as a digital nomad requires a clear understanding of the expectations and responsibilities associated with each assignment. This guide will help you identify and manage your responsibilities, ensuring you provide excellent service and maintain a positive reputation within the house and pet sitting community.

1. Read the homeowner's listing carefully:
   - Before accepting a house or pet sitting assignment, read the homeowner's listing thoroughly to gain a clear understanding of their specific needs and expectations.
   - Take note of any special instructions, routines, or preferences they mention, as these details will help you tailor your approach to meet their requirements.

2. Communicate with the homeowner:
   - Establish open and honest communication with the homeowner to discuss their expectations and any concerns or questions you may have. This can help to clarify your responsibilities and ensure that you are both on the same page regarding the assignment.

3. Create a checklist of responsibilities:
   - Develop a comprehensive checklist of tasks and responsibilities associated with the assignment, including pet care, home maintenance, and any additional requests from the homeowner. This will help you stay organized and ensure that you do not overlook any important tasks.

4. Prioritize tasks and create a schedule:
   - Prioritize your tasks based on the homeowner's preferences and the urgency of each responsibility.
   - Create a daily or weekly schedule to help you manage your time effectively and ensure that all tasks are completed in a timely manner.

5. Be prepared for emergencies:
   - Familiarize yourself with the location of emergency supplies, such as first aid kits, fire extinguishers, and emergency contact numbers for the homeowner, veterinarian, and local authorities.
   - Develop a plan for handling emergencies, such as power outages, medical issues, or natural disasters, and discuss this plan with the homeowner.

6. Maintain regular communication with the homeowner:
   - Keep the homeowner informed of any updates, changes, or issues that arise during the assignment. Regular communication helps to build trust and reassures the homeowner that their home and pets are being well-cared for in their absence.

7. Document any issues or damage:
   - If any issues or damage occur during the assignment, document the situation with photos and detailed notes. Communicate this information to the homeowner promptly and discuss any necessary steps to address the issue.

8. Respect the homeowner's privacy and property:
   - Treat the homeowner's home and belongings with respect and adhere to any rules or guidelines they have provided. Avoid using their personal items or entering restricted areas without permission.

9. Be adaptable and resourceful:
   - As a digital nomad, you may encounter unexpected challenges or changes in your house or pet sitting assignment. Be prepared to adapt and find creative solutions to these situations, demonstrating your resourcefulness and commitment to providing excellent service.

10. Leave the home clean and tidy:
   - Before departing from the assignment, ensure that the home is clean and tidy, with all tasks completed to the homeowner's satisfaction. This will help to leave a positive impression and increase the likelihood of receiving positive reviews and future assignments.

Maintain a positive reputation

Maintaining a positive reputation is essential for digital nomads looking to become successful house or pet sitters. A powerful reputation will help you secure more assignments and build trust with homeowners. This guide will provide tips on how to maintain a positive reputation within the house and pet sitting community.

1. Provide exceptional service:
   - Go beyond to provide excellent service to homeowners and their pets. This includes following instructions, being punctual, and proactively addressing any issues that may arise.
   - A strong work ethic and attention to detail will help you stand out and leave a positive impression on homeowners.

2. Be honest and transparent:
   - Establish open and honest communication with homeowners from the outset. This includes discussing your qualifications, experience, and any potential limitations or concerns.
   - Transparency helps to build trust and sets a sturdy foundation for a successful house or pet sitting assignment.

3. Maintain professionalism:
   - Always maintain a professional demeanour when interacting with homeowners, both online and in person.
   - Be respectful, polite, and courteous, and adhere to any guidelines or rules set by the homeowner.

4. Collect positive reviews and testimonials:
   - Encourage homeowners to provide reviews or testimonials after each assignment. Positive feedback can help bolster your reputation and attract more clients.
   - Share these reviews on your online profiles and website to showcase your skills and experience.

5. Respond to feedback:
   - Take the time to respond to feedback, both positive and negative, in a professional and courteous manner. Thank homeowners for their reviews and use any constructive criticism as an opportunity to learn and improve your services.

6. Network within the community:
   - Connect with other house and pet sitters, as well as homeowners, to share experiences, advice, and resources. Networking within the community can help you learn from others, build connections, and enhance your reputation.

7. Maintain a strong online presence:
   - Keep your online profiles, website, and social media accounts up to date and professional. Showcase your skills, experience, and positive reviews to attract potential clients.
   - Engage with your audience and share relevant content to demonstrate your expertise in the field.

8. Stay organized and reliable:
   - Ensure that you are well-prepared for each assignment by organizing your travel arrangements, documentation, and communication with homeowners.
   - Reliability and organization will help to demonstrate your commitment to providing excellent service and leave a positive impression on homeowners.

9. Continue to develop your skills:
   - Invest in ongoing professional development by attending workshops, courses, or webinars related to house or pet sitting.
   - Staying current with best practices and industry trends will help you maintain an elevated level of service and demonstrate your dedication to your craft.

10. Resolve conflicts professionally:
   - If a conflict or issue arises with a homeowner, approach the situation professionally and calmly. Seek to understand the homeowner's concerns and work together to find a resolution.
   - Demonstrating your ability to handle challenging situations in a mature and professional manner can help maintain your positive reputation.

VIRTUAL ASSISTANT

The digital nomad lifestyle offers freedom and flexibility, making it an ideal choice for those who crave adventure while working remotely. As a virtual assistant, you can provide administrative support for businesses and enjoy the rewards of a location-independent career. This comprehensive guide will help you establish yourself as a successful digital nomad virtual assistant.

Assess your skills and interests

Assessing your skills and interests is a critical step in becoming a successful digital nomad virtual assistant. By following the tips outlined in this guide, you can identify your unique strengths, develop a service offering, and set yourself on the path to success in the virtual assistant industry.

1. Make a list of your skills:
   - Begin by making a comprehensive list of your current skills, including both hard and soft skills.
   - Hard skills may include proficiency in software programs, data entry, social media management, or graphic design.
   - Soft skills can encompass communication, time management, and problem-solving abilities.

2. Identify your interests and passions:
- In addition to your skills, consider your interests and passions. Working in areas that genuinely interest you can lead to higher job satisfaction and better performance. Think about the industries, tasks, or subject areas that you enjoy and consider how they might align with your skills.

3. Determine your strengths:
- Reflect on your past experiences and identify the tasks or projects where you excelled. Your strengths can guide you in choosing the services you want to offer as a virtual assistant.
- Focus on tasks that showcase your skills and align with your interests.

4. Research the market demand:
- Research the virtual assistant market to understand the most in-demand services. This can help you identify potential niches and opportunities for your skill set.
- Keep in mind that while it is essential to consider market demand, it is also crucial to focus on areas where you have the skills and passion to succeed.

5. Obtain feedback from others:
- Ask friends, family, or former colleagues for feedback on your strengths and weaknesses. This can provide valuable insights into areas where you excel and where you might need improvement.
- Use this feedback to refine your list of skills and focus on the areas where you shine.

6. Consider additional training or certifications:
- If you discover gaps in your skills or areas where you would like to improve, consider investing in additional training or certifications.
- Online courses, workshops, and certifications can help you develop new skills or strengthen existing ones, making you a more competitive candidate in the virtual assistant market.

7. Match your skills to potential services:
- With a thorough understanding of your skills, interests, and market demand, begin matching your abilities to potential services you can offer as a virtual assistant. This may include administrative tasks, social media management, content creation, or project management, depending on your unique skill set.

8. Create a service offering:
- Compile a list of services you can confidently offer based on your skills and interests. Be specific in detailing the tasks you can perform and any relevant experience or certifications you possess. This will serve as the foundation for your virtual assistant business.

Develop your skillset

To succeed as a virtual assistant, you will need a diverse range of skills to meet various client needs. This guide will provide tips and resources to help you develop your skillset and excel in the virtual assistant industry.

1. General administrative tasks (email management, scheduling, data entry):

- Familiarize yourself with popular email clients and productivity tools such as Gmail, Outlook, and Google Workspace.
- Learn to use scheduling tools like Google Calendar, Microsoft Outlook Calendar, or Calendly to manage appointments and deadlines.
- Practice data entry and spreadsheet management using Microsoft Excel, Google Sheets, or similar tools.

2. Project management and coordination:
   - Gain a basic understanding of project management methodologies, such as Agile or Waterfall, through online courses or books.
   - Familiarize yourself with project management tools like Trello, Asana, Basecamp, or Monday.com to manage tasks and timelines.
   - Develop your time management and organizational skills to ensure smooth project coordination.

3. Customer service and communication:

   - Enhance your written and verbal communication skills by taking courses, reading books, or participating in online forums.
   - Learn techniques for effective customer service, including active listening, empathy, and problem-solving.
   - Practice using communication tools such as Slack, Microsoft Teams, or Zoom to collaborate with clients or team members.

4. Social media management and marketing:

   - Stay up to date with the latest social media platforms, trends, and best practices by following industry blogs or participating in online communities.
   - Learn to use social media management tools like Hootsuite, Buffer, or Sprout Social to schedule posts and monitor engagement.
   - Develop a basic understanding of social media advertising on platforms such as Facebook, Instagram, or LinkedIn to assist with marketing efforts.

5. Basic graphic design and content creation:

   - Familiarize yourself with design principles and tools like Adobe Creative Suite, Canva, or GIMP for graphic design tasks.
   - Learn basic video editing techniques using software like Adobe Premiere Pro, Final Cut Pro, or iMovie.
   - Develop your writing skills by taking courses, participating in writing workshops, or practicing on your blog.

Resources for Skill Development:
- Online courses: Platforms like Coursera, Udemy, and LinkedIn Learning offer a variety of courses to help you develop new skills or enhance existing ones.
- Books and eBooks: Look for books, eBooks, or audiobooks on relevant topics to deepen your understanding of various skills.
- Blogs and YouTube channels: Follow industry blogs and YouTube channels for updates, tips, and tutorials on specific skills.
- Online communities and forums: Participate in relevant online communities and forums to learn from others, ask questions, and share experiences.

Build a professional online presence

Building a professional online presence is crucial for attracting clients and establishing yourself as a successful digital nomad virtual assistant. By following the tips outlined in this guide, you will create a strong and consistent online presence that sets you apart in the competitive virtual assistance market.

1. Create a professional website:

- Design a clean, user-friendly website that highlights your services, skills, and experience. Include a portfolio, client testimonials, and a blog to showcase your expertise.
- Optimize your website for SEO to increase visibility in search engine results.
- Ensure your website is mobile-responsive, as many clients will view your site on their smartphones or tablets.

2. Develop a consistent brand identity:

- Choose a professional name or business name that reflects your services and expertise.
- Create a consistent brand identity, including a logo, colour scheme, and typography, to use across your website and social media profiles.
- Ensure your branding reflects your target market and the services you provide.

3. Set up professional social media profiles:

- Create dedicated social media profiles for your virtual assistant business on platforms such as LinkedIn, Facebook, and Instagram.
- Use your consistent branding across all social media profiles.
- Share valuable content, engage with your audience, and showcase your expertise on your social media platforms.

4. Join online communities and forums:

- Participate in online communities and forums related to virtual assistance, freelancing, and your specific niche or industry.
- Engage with other professionals, ask questions, and share your knowledge and experience.
- Building relationships in these communities can lead to referrals and networking opportunities.

5. Maintain a professional blog:

- Regularly publish blog posts related to your niche or industry to demonstrate your expertise and knowledge.
- Share tips, tutorials, and case studies that are relevant to your target audience.
- Promote your blog posts on your social media profiles and within online communities to increase visibility and engagement.

6. Showcase your portfolio and testimonials:

- Highlight your best work and client projects in a dedicated portfolio section on your website.
- Include testimonials from satisfied clients to provide social proof of your skills and reliability.
- Update your portfolio and testimonials regularly as you complete new projects and receive additional feedback.

7. Optimise your LinkedIn profile:

- Complete your LinkedIn profile with a professional photo, headline, summary, and detailed work experience.
- Request endorsements and recommendations from colleagues, clients, and peers.
- Engage with your network and share relevant content to showcase your expertise and stay top of mind.

8. Determine your niche and services

Specializing in a specific niche or offering a unique set of services can set you apart from the competition. Determine what type of clients you want to work with and what services you want to offer based on your skills and interests.

9. Set your rates

Establish competitive rates for your services based on your experience, expertise, and the industry standard. Consider whether to charge per hour, per project, or on a retainer basis, and be prepared to negotiate with clients to reach a fair agreement.

Find clients and build your network

There are several ways to find clients as a digital nomad virtual assistant, including:

- Freelance platforms like Upwork, Freelancer, or Fiverr
- Job boards and virtual assistant-specific websites
- Networking on social media and within virtual assistant communities
- Word-of-mouth referrals from satisfied clients

Create a system for managing tasks and deadlines

Creating an effective system for managing tasks and deadlines is crucial for a successful virtual assistant career. By following the tips outlined in this guide, you will develop a reliable and efficient system that helps you stay organized, prioritize tasks, and meet deadlines, leading to satisfied clients and a thriving digital nomad lifestyle.

1. Choose a task management tool:
   - Explore task management tools such as Asana, Trello, or Todoist to help you organize and prioritize your tasks.
   - Consider the features you need, such as collaboration, calendar integration, and mobile access when selecting a tool.
   - Stick with one tool that works best for you to avoid confusion and maintain consistency.

2. Develop a daily routine:
   - Establish a daily routine that includes time for checking emails, updating your task list, and completing high-priority tasks.
   - Set aside dedicated time for each client or project to ensure you are giving them the attention they deserve.
   - Review your tasks at the end of each day and update your task list accordingly.

3. Prioritize tasks:
   - Use a prioritization method, such as the Eisenhower Matrix or the ABCDE method, to categorize tasks based on urgency and importance.
   - Focus on completing high-priority tasks before moving on to less urgent or important tasks.
   - Re-evaluate your priorities regularly as new tasks and deadlines arise.

4. Set realistic deadlines:
   - When setting deadlines for tasks, consider factors such as complexity, client expectations, and your current workload.
   - Be realistic about how long a task will take and build in a buffer to accommodate unforeseen issues.
   - Communicate your deadlines with clients and set expectations accordingly.

5. Break tasks into smaller steps:
   - Break down complex tasks into smaller, more manageable steps to make them less overwhelming.
   - Assign deadlines for each step to keep yourself on track and ensure timely completion of the overall task.
   - Use your task management tool to create subtasks or checklists to track your progress.

6. Use a calendar system:
   - Sync your task management tool with a calendar system, such as Google Calendar or Outlook Calendar, to visualize deadlines and stay organized.
   - Schedule dedicated time blocks for specific tasks or projects to help you stay focused and maintain productivity.
   - Set reminders for important deadlines to ensure you stay on track.

7. Regularly review and adjust:
   - Regularly review your task list and calendar to ensure you are staying on top of your workload and making necessary adjustments.
   - Update your task list and deadlines as needed to accommodate new tasks, changing priorities, or unexpected delays.
   - Communicate any changes in deadlines or workload with your clients promptly.

Maintain clear communication with clients

Clear communication is essential for a successful virtual assistant career. It helps build trust, manage expectations, and ensure smooth project execution. This guide will provide tips for maintaining clear communication with clients, even as a digital nomad working remotely.

1. Set communication expectations:
   - Discuss communication preferences with your clients during the onboarding process, including preferred communication channels, response times, and frequency of updates.

- Establish guidelines for urgent matters, such as how to reach you during non-working hours or preferred channels for urgent communication.
- Be upfront about your working hours, time zone differences, and any planned vacations or absences.

2. Choose reliable communication tools:
   - Utilize reliable communication tools, such as email, video conferencing (e.g., Zoom or Skype), and instant messaging (e.g., Slack or Microsoft Teams).
   - Ensure that you have a stable internet connection and backup communication options when traveling as a digital nomad.
   - Familiarize yourself with your clients' preferred communication tools and adapt your communication style accordingly.

3. Provide regular updates and progress reports:
   - Keep clients informed about your progress on tasks and projects by providing regular updates and progress reports.
   - Proactively communicate any challenges or delays that may impact deadlines or project outcomes.
   - Be transparent about your workload and capacity, especially when juggling multiple clients or projects.

4. Listen actively and ask questions:
   - Practice active listening when communicating with clients to ensure you fully understand their needs and expectations.
   - Do not be afraid to ask questions or seek clarification if you are unsure about any aspect of a project or task.
   - Repeat vital information or instructions back to the client to confirm your understanding and avoid miscommunications.

5. Be professional and concise:
   - Maintain a professional tone in all written and verbal communication with clients.
   - Keep your messages clear and concise, focusing on essential information and avoiding unnecessary jargon.
   - Use proper grammar, spelling, and punctuation to ensure your messages are easily understood.

6. Respond promptly to client inquiries:
   - Respond to client inquiries and messages in a timely manner, adhering to the response time expectations you have established.
   - If you are unable to address a client's inquiry immediately, send a brief acknowledgment and let them know when you will be able to provide a more detailed response.
   - Stay organized by keeping track of ongoing conversations and following up on any outstanding issues or requests.

7. Request feedback and encourage open communication:
   - Encourage clients to provide feedback on your work and communication style and be open to adjusting as needed.
   - Foster an open communication environment by being approachable and receptive to questions, concerns, or suggestions from clients.
   - Regularly check in with clients to ensure they are satisfied with your work and communication.

Continuously improve your skills

Continuously improving your skills is essential for staying competitive and successful as a digital nomad virtual assistant. By following the tips outlined in this guide, you will develop a growth mindset and proactively enhance your expertise, ensuring you stay relevant and valuable to your clients. This commitment to growth will lead to a thriving virtual assistant career and a fulfilling digital nomad lifestyle.

1. Identify skill gaps and growth areas:
   - Assess your current skill set and identify areas where you could improve or expand your expertise.
   - Consider the specific needs of your clients and target market to determine which skills would be most valuable to develop.

2. Pursue relevant online courses and certifications:
   - Take advantage of online learning platforms like Coursera, Udemy, or LinkedIn Learning to access a wide range of courses and certifications.
   - Choose courses that align with your growth areas and the needs of your clients.
   - Consider obtaining certifications to validate your expertise and stand out from the competition.

3. Attend webinars, workshops, and conferences:
   - Participate in webinars, workshops, and conferences within your industry or areas of interest to learn from experts and stay current with trends.
   - Look for both in-person and virtual events that cater to digital nomads and remote workers.
   - Network with other professionals to share knowledge, experiences, and best practices.

4. Join professional communities and forums:
   - Engage with online communities and forums dedicated to virtual assistants or your areas of expertise to exchange ideas, resources, and tips.
   - Participate in discussions, ask questions, and share your own insights to learn from others and contribute to the community.
   - Look for niche communities that cater to specific industries or client types, such as small business owners or entrepreneurs.

5. Stay updated with industry news and trends:
   - Subscribe to newsletters, blogs, or podcasts that cover industry news, trends, and best practices.
   - Dedicate time each week to reading or listening to relevant content to stay informed and inspired.
   - Implement new tools, techniques, or strategies you learn about to improve your work as a virtual assistant.

6. Seek feedback from clients and peers:
   - Request feedback from clients on your work, communication, and overall performance.
   - Be open to constructive criticism and use it as an opportunity to grow and improve.
   - Reach out to fellow virtual assistants or industry peers for advice, mentorship, or skill-sharing opportunities.

7. Practice self-reflection and goal setting:
   - Regularly evaluate your progress, accomplishments, and areas for improvement through self-reflection.
   - Set short-term and long-term goals for skill development and professional growth.
   - Review and adjust your goals as needed to ensure they remain relevant and attainable.

SOCIAL MEDIA MARKETING

The digital nomad lifestyle offers the opportunity to travel the world while working remotely. As a social media marketer, you can help businesses grow their online presence and thrive in the digital age. This comprehensive guide will help you establish yourself as a successful digital nomad social media marketer.

Assess your skills and interests

Assessing your skills and interests is a critical step in becoming a successful digital nomad virtual assistant. By following the tips outlined in this guide, you can identify your unique strengths, develop a service offering, and set yourself on the path to success in the virtual assistant industry.

1. Make a list of your skills:
   - Begin by making a comprehensive list of your current skills, including both hard and soft skills.
   - Hard skills may include proficiency in software programs, data entry, social media management, or graphic design.
   - Soft skills can encompass communication, time management, and problem-solving abilities.

2. Identify your interests and passions:
   - In addition to your skills, consider your interests and passions. Working in areas that genuinely interest you can lead to higher job satisfaction and better performance.
   - Think about the industries, tasks, or subject areas that you enjoy and consider how they might align with your skills.

3. Determine your strengths:
   - Reflect on your past experiences and identify the tasks or projects where you excelled. Your strengths can guide you in choosing the services you want to offer as a virtual assistant. Focus on tasks that showcase your skills and align with your interests.

4. Research the market demand:
   - Research the virtual assistant market to understand the most in-demand services. This can help you identify potential niches and opportunities for your skill set. Keep in mind that while it is essential to consider market demand, it is also crucial to focus on areas where you have the skills and passion to succeed.

5. Obtain feedback from others:
   - Ask friends, family, or former colleagues for feedback on your strengths and weaknesses. This can provide valuable insights into areas where you excel and where you might need improvement.
   - Use this feedback to refine your list of skills and focus on the areas where you shine.

6. Consider additional training or certifications:
   - If you discover gaps in your skills or areas where you would like to improve, consider investing in additional training or certifications.
   - Online courses, workshops, and certifications can help you develop new skills or strengthen existing ones, making you a more competitive candidate in the virtual assistant market.

7. Match your skills to potential services:
   - With a thorough understanding of your skills, interests, and market demand, begin matching your abilities to potential services you can offer as a virtual assistant.
   - This may include administrative tasks, social media management, content creation, or project management, depending on your unique skill set.

8. Create a service offering:
   - Compile a list of services you can confidently offer based on your skills and interests. Be specific in detailing the tasks you can perform and any relevant experience or certifications you possess. This will serve as the foundation for your virtual assistant business.

Develop your skillset to be a successful social media marketer

Assessing your skills and interests is a critical step in becoming a successful digital nomad virtual assistant. By following the tips outlined in this guide, you can identify your unique strengths, develop a service offering, and set yourself on the path to success in the virtual assistant industry.

1. Make a list of your skills:
   - Begin by making a comprehensive list of your current skills, including both hard and soft skills.
   - Hard skills may include proficiency in software programs, data entry, social media management, or graphic design.
   - Soft skills can encompass communication, time management, and problem-solving abilities.

2. Identify your interests and passions:
   - In addition to your skills, consider your interests and passions. Working in areas that genuinely interest you can lead to higher job satisfaction and better performance.
   - Think about the industries, tasks, or subject areas that you enjoy and consider how they might align with your skills.

3. Determine your strengths:
   - Reflect on your past experiences and identify the tasks or projects where you excelled. Your strengths can guide you in choosing the services you want to offer as a virtual assistant.
   - Focus on tasks that showcase your skills and align with your interests.

4. Research the market demand:
   - Research the virtual assistant market to understand the most in-demand services. This can help you identify potential niches and opportunities for your skill set.
   - Keep in mind that while it is essential to consider market demand, it is also crucial to focus on areas where you have the skills and passion to succeed.

5. Obtain feedback from others:
   - Ask friends, family, or former colleagues for feedback on your strengths and weaknesses. This can provide valuable insights into areas where you excel and where you might need improvement.
   - Use this feedback to refine your list of skills and focus on the areas where you shine.

6. Consider additional training or certifications:
   - If you discover gaps in your skills or areas where you would like to improve, consider investing in additional training or certifications.
   - Online courses, workshops, and certifications can help you develop new skills or strengthen existing ones, making you a more competitive candidate in the virtual assistant market.

7. Match your skills to potential services:
   - With a thorough understanding of your skills, interests, and market demand, begin matching your abilities to potential services you can offer as a virtual assistant.
   - This may include administrative tasks, social media management, content creation, or project management, depending on your unique skill set.

8. Create a service offering:
   - Compile a list of services you can confidently offer based on your skills and interests. Be specific in detailing the tasks you can perform and any relevant experience or certifications you possess. This will serve as the foundation for your virtual assistant business.

Build a professional online presence

To become successful social media marketers, establishing a strong online presence is essential to attract clients and showcase your skills. In this guide, we will discuss the steps you can take to create a solid online presence that reflects your expertise as a social media marketer.

1. Create a professional website:
   - Choose a domain name that represents your personal brand or business name.
   - Design a clean, easy-to-navigate website that highlights your skills, services, portfolio, testimonials, and contact information.
   - Keep your website up to date with fresh content, such as blog posts, case studies, or industry news.

2. Establish a presence on social media platforms:
   - Create profiles on LinkedIn, Facebook, Instagram, and Twitter, ensuring they are consistently branded and visually appealing.
   - Use these platforms to showcase your social media marketing skills, share relevant content, and engage with your audience.
   - Consistently post updates on your projects, achievements, and industry insights to demonstrate your expertise and maintain visibility.

3. Join social media marketing communities and forums:
   - Participate in online communities, such as Reddit, Quora, or specialized forums, where professionals discuss social media marketing trends and strategies.
   - Offer valuable insights, ask questions, and share your experiences to establish credibility and build relationships with fellow marketers and potential clients.

4. Network with industry professionals:
   - Attend industry events, webinars, and conferences to connect with other social media marketers, potential clients, and influencers in your niche.
   - Collaborate with fellow professionals on projects, guest posts, or content sharing to expand your reach and gain exposure.

5. Optimize your online presence for search engines:
   - Use search engine optimization (SEO) techniques to improve your website's visibility on search engine results pages.
   - Research relevant keywords and incorporate them into your website's content, meta tags, and image descriptions.
   - Build high-quality backlinks to your website by guest posting, collaborating with industry professionals, or engaging in social media marketing communities.

Determine your niche and services

Specializing in a specific niche or offering a unique set of services can help set you apart from the competition. In this guide, we will discuss how to determine your ideal clients and the services you want to offer based on your skills and interests.

1. Assess your skills and interests:
   - Make a list of your social media marketing skills, such as content creation, analytics, strategy development, or ad management.
   - Consider your passions and interests outside of social media marketing, as they may help you identify a niche, you would enjoy working in.

2. Identify your target audience:
   - Research different industries or market segments that align with your skills and interests.

- Determine the types of businesses, organizations, or individuals you would like to work with, such as startups, nonprofits, e-commerce, or personal brands.

4. Define your niche and unique selling proposition (USP):
   - Based on your target audience and the services you want to offer, identify a niche that allows you to differentiate yourself from other social media marketers.
   - Develop a USP that highlights your unique skills, expertise, or approach to social media marketing within your chosen niche.

5. Tailor your services to your niche:
   - Create a list of services that cater specifically to the needs of your target audience within your chosen niche.
   - Focus on offering high-quality, specialized services that showcase your expertise and provide value to your clients.

6. Promote your niche expertise:
   - Update your website, social media profiles, and marketing materials to reflect your specialization and USP.
   - Share content, case studies, and testimonials that demonstrate your success and expertise within your niche.
   - Network with industry professionals and potential clients within your niche to build relationships and increase your visibility.

7. Continuously improve your skills and knowledge:
   - Stay up to date with the latest trends, tools, and best practices within your niche to ensure you remain competitive and relevant.
   - Attend webinars, conferences, and workshops focused on your niche, and participate in online forums and communities to expand your knowledge.

Set your rates

Setting competitive rates is essential for digital nomads building a successful social media marketing career. In this guide, we will explore how to establish rates based on your experience, expertise, and industry standards, as well as discuss different pricing structures.

1. Research industry standards:
   - Investigate the average rates for social media marketing services within your chosen niche and region.
   - Take note of the pricing structures used by competitors and successful marketers in your field.

2. Evaluate your experience and expertise:
   - Assess your level of experience and the unique skills you bring to the table.
   - Determine how your expertise and qualifications compare to others in your niche and adjust your rates accordingly.

3. Choose a pricing structure:
   - Consider charging per hour, per project, or on a retainer basis. Each method has its pros and cons, so weigh your options carefully.
   - Hourly rates: Suitable for smaller projects or tasks with variable time requirements.

- Project-based rates: Suitable for larger projects with a clearly defined scope and timeline.
- Retainer fees: Suitable for ongoing work or clients who require consistent support and availability.

4. Set your rates:
   - Based on your research and self-assessment, establish competitive rates for your services.
   - Ensure that your rates are fair to both you and your clients, covering your costs and providing room for profit.

5. Be prepared to negotiate:
   - Recognize that some clients may want to negotiate rates. Be prepared to discuss and potentially adjust your pricing while maintaining a fair agreement.
   - Develop a strategy for handling negotiation requests, such as offering discounts for long-term contracts or bundling services.

6. Review and adjust your rates periodically:
   - Regularly evaluate your rates to ensure they remain competitive and reflect your current experience and expertise.
   - As your skills and client base grow, do not be afraid to raise your rates accordingly.

Find clients and build your network

Finding clients is key to achieving financial independence and stability. In this guide, we will discuss various methods to find clients for your social media marketing services.

1. Freelance platforms:
   - Sign up for popular freelance platforms such as Upwork, Freelancer, and Fiverr.
   - Create a strong profile showcasing your skills, experience, and portfolio.
   - Search for social media marketing projects and submit proposals to potential clients.

2. Job boards and niche websites:
   - Browse job boards, such as Indeed, Glassdoor, and SimplyHired, for social media marketing opportunities.
   - Explore niche websites dedicated to social media marketing jobs, such as SocialMediaJobs.com or Mediabistro.
   - Apply for relevant positions and showcase your expertise in your cover letter and resume.

3. Networking on social media and marketing communities:
   - Use social media platforms, like LinkedIn, Facebook, and Twitter, to connect with professionals in your niche and potential clients.
   - Join social media marketing groups and communities to network with fellow marketers, share your expertise, and learn about job opportunities.
   - Attend industry events, conferences, and webinars to expand your network and gain valuable insights.

4. Word-of-mouth referrals:
   - Provide exceptional service to your clients, ensuring their satisfaction and fostering long-term relationships.

- Encourage satisfied clients to recommend your services to their network, boosting your reputation and potential client base.
- Offer incentives, such as discounts or referral bonuses, for clients who refer new business to you.

5. Develop strategic partnerships:
   - Collaborate with complementary businesses, such as web designers, content creators, or SEO specialists, to offer comprehensive digital marketing services.
   - Leverage these partnerships to gain access to new clients and expand your service offerings.

6. Create valuable content:
   - Develop and share informative blog posts, articles, or social media updates related to social media marketing.
   - Showcase your knowledge and expertise, positioning yourself as a thought leader in your niche.
   - Attract potential clients who are interested in your insights and require social media marketing services.

Create a system for managing tasks and deadlines

As a digital nomad social media marketer, staying organized is essential for delivering projects on time and maintaining client satisfaction. In this guide, we will discuss how to use project management tools to plan, schedule, and track social media content and campaigns efficiently.

1. Choose the right project management tool:
   - Select a project management tool that suits your needs and preferences. Popular options include Trello, Asana, and ContentCal.
   - Compare features, pricing, and ease of use to determine the best fit for your workflow.

2. Set up your workspace:
   - Create a dedicated workspace within your chosen project management tool for each client or project.
   - Organize tasks and content by category, campaign, or platform to streamline your workflow.

3. Plan and schedule content:
   - Develop a content calendar outlining the type of content, posting dates, and target platforms for each piece.
   - Use your project management tool to create tasks or cards for each piece of content, including relevant information such as captions, hashtags, images, or links.
   - Set deadlines for content creation, editing, and scheduling to stay on track and ensure timely delivery.

4. Track progress and deadlines:
   - Use your project management tool's features, such as checklists, labels, or progress bars, to monitor the status of each task or content piece.
   - Set reminders or notifications to ensure you do not miss any deadlines or important updates.

5. Collaborate with clients and team members:
   - Invite clients or team members to your project management workspace to facilitate communication, feedback, and collaboration.
   - Use features like comments, file sharing, or task assignments to streamline the content creation and approval process.

6. Review and analyse results:
   - Monitor the performance of your social media content and campaigns, tracking metrics such as engagement, reach, and conversions.
   - Use your project management tool to store performance data and insights for future reference and optimization.

7. Continuously optimize your workflow:
   - Regularly review your project management process to identify areas for improvement or potential bottlenecks.
   - Implement changes to your workflow, such as adjusting your content calendar or task organization, to increase efficiency and productivity.

Maintain clear communication with clients

Clear and consistent communication is essential for building strong relationships with your clients as a digital nomad social media marketer. In this guide, we will discuss how to establish regular check-ins, provide status updates, and address concerns proactively to maintain client satisfaction.

1. Set clear expectations from the start:
   - Discuss your clients' goals, target audience, and preferred communication channels during the onboarding process.
   - Outline the scope of work, timelines, and deliverables to ensure both parties have a mutual understanding.

2. Establish regular check-ins:
   - Schedule periodic check-ins with your clients, such as weekly or monthly meetings, to discuss progress and address any questions or concerns.
   - Use video conferencing tools like Zoom or Skype to maintain a personal connection, especially when working remotely.

3. Provide status updates on your work:
   - Keep your clients informed about the progress of social media campaigns, content creation, and any relevant metrics or results.
   - Use your project management tool to share updates or create brief reports to summarize your work and achievements.

4. Be responsive to client needs:
   - Respond to client inquiries, feedback, or requests in a timely manner to demonstrate your commitment to their success.
   - Be flexible and adaptable to accommodate any changes in project scope or priorities.

5. Address concerns or issues proactively:
   - If you encounter challenges or obstacles in your work, communicate these to your clients and propose solutions to resolve them.

- Encourage open and honest feedback from your clients to identify areas for improvement and maintain a strong working relationship.

6. Offer value-added services:
   - Look for opportunities to go beyond your clients' expectations by offering additional insights, suggestions, or resources related to their social media marketing goals.
   - Share industry news, trends, or best practices to demonstrate your expertise and commitment to their success.

7. Ask for testimonials and referrals:
   - Once you have successfully completed a project or campaign, ask your satisfied clients for testimonials or referrals to help build your reputation and attract new clients.

Continuously improve your skills

As a digital nomad social media marketer, it is essential to stay competitive in the ever-evolving landscape of social media marketing. In this guide, we will discuss how to regularly update and expand your skillset through online courses, webinars, and industry events.

1. Take online courses:
   - Enrol in online courses to learn new skills and stay up to date on social media marketing trends and strategies.
   - Platforms like Coursera, Udemy, and LinkedIn Learning offer a wide range of courses in social media marketing, content creation, and analytics.

2. Attend webinars and virtual workshops:
   - Participate in webinars and virtual workshops hosted by industry experts to gain insights into the latest social media marketing techniques and tools.
   - Join mailing lists, follow industry influencers, and subscribe to marketing blogs to stay informed about upcoming webinars.

3. Participate in industry events and conferences:
   - Attend virtual or in-person social media marketing events and conferences to network with other professionals, learn from experts, and discover emerging trends.
   - Look for events organized by industry associations or platforms like Social Media Examiner, Social Media Week, or Social Media Marketing World.

4. Obtain certifications:
   - Pursue professional certifications from reputable organizations like Facebook Blueprint, Google Ads, or Hootsuite Academy to validate your skills and enhance your credibility.
   - Certifications can help you stand out from the competition and may lead to more job opportunities or higher rates.

5. Join online communities and forums:
   - Engage with fellow social media marketers through online communities and forums, such as Facebook or LinkedIn groups, Reddit, or Quora.
   - Share your experiences, ask questions, and learn from others to continuously improve your skills and knowledge.

6. Stay informed on industry news and trends:

- Regularly read social media marketing blogs, newsletters, and publications to stay informed about industry news, trends, and best practices.
- Subscribe to sources like Social Media Examiner, Buffer, or Sprout Social for valuable insights and updates.

7. Collaborate and learn from peers:
   - Connect with other digital nomad social media marketers to exchange ideas, learn from their experiences, and stay motivated in your career.
   - Consider partnering on projects or forming mastermind groups to support each other's growth and success.

TRANSCRIPTION WORK

The digital nomad lifestyle offers the freedom to travel the world while working remotely. As a transcriptionist, you can convert audio content into written text, providing valuable services to businesses and professionals. By specializing in fields like medical transcription, you can earn higher pay while enjoying the rewards of a location-independent career. This comprehensive guide will help you establish yourself as a successful digital nomad transcriptionist.

Assess your skills and interests

Working as a digital nomad transcriptionist can be an excellent career choice for those with strong typing skills and attention to detail. Before embarking on this journey, it is essential to assess your skills and determine if transcription is the right fit for you. This guide will help you evaluate your abilities by asking the following questions:

1. Do you have strong typing skills and a keen ear for detail? Transcriptionists need to accurately convert spoken words into written text. To be successful in this field, consider the following:
   - Assess your typing speed and accuracy. A minimum of sixty words per minute (WPM) with high accuracy is typically required for most transcription jobs.
   - Evaluate your listening skills, as you will need to understand and accurately transcribe various speakers, even in less-than-ideal audio quality.

2. Are you comfortable working with various accents and dialects? Transcription work often involves transcribing audio from speakers with diverse accents and dialects. To assess your comfort level:
   - Listen to sample audio files featuring speakers with different accents to gauge your ability to understand and transcribe their speech.
   - Consider taking courses or practicing with language resources to improve your understanding of various accents and dialects.

3. Can you maintain focus and accuracy while working on repetitive tasks? Transcription work can be repetitive, requiring sustained attention and focus to ensure accurate transcriptions. To determine if you can handle this aspect of the job:
   - Reflect on your experience with repetitive tasks and your ability to maintain focus and accuracy over extended periods.

- Practice transcribing long audio files to see if you can maintain consistent performance throughout the task.

4. Are you comfortable working remotely and maintaining a reliable internet connection? As a digital nomad, you will need to work from various locations and ensure a stable internet connection. To assess your comfort with remote work:
   - Evaluate your experience working remotely and your ability to stay productive and organized without direct supervision.
   - Research the internet requirements for transcription work and ensure you can maintain a stable connection in your chosen destinations.

Develop your skillset to be a successful transcriptionist

To thrive as a digital nomad transcriptionist, you need to develop a range of skills that will help you deliver accurate transcriptions and stand out in the industry. This guide will provide you with an overview of the essential skills needed for a successful career in transcription and tips on how to develop them.

1. Fast and accurate typing:
   - Practice your typing skills extensively using online typing tests and tools like Typing.com or 10FastFingers to improve your speed and accuracy.
   - Use keyboard shortcuts and touch-typing techniques to increase efficiency and reduce errors.

2. Active listening and comprehension:
   - Enhance your listening skills by transcribing several types of audio, including interviews, podcasts, and videos with diverse accents, dialects, and audio quality.
   - Develop your ability to concentrate for extended periods by practicing mindfulness exercises and taking regular breaks.

3. Proofreading and editing:
   - Improve your grammar, punctuation, and spelling by taking online courses or using resources like Grammarly and Hemingway Editor.
   - Practice proofreading your transcriptions and develop a systematic approach to ensure consistency and accuracy.

4. Familiarity with transcription software and tools:
   - Explore different transcription software, such as Express Scribe or InqScribe, and choose the one that best fits your needs.
   - Learn how to use transcription-specific tools like foot pedals, text expanders, and noise-cancellation headphones to enhance your productivity and comfort.

Gain experience and certifications

To succeed as a digital nomad transcriptionist, it is crucial to build a strong resume that showcases your experience, skills, and certifications. This guide will provide you with steps to build a solid transcription resume and enhance your credibility in the industry.

1. Gain experience through internships and entry-level positions:

- Look for internships or entry-level transcription positions to gain valuable hands-on experience.
- Seek opportunities in different industries, such as legal, medical, or general transcription, to diversify your skill set.

2. Start with freelance work:
   - Register on freelance platforms like Upwork, Freelancer, or Rev to find transcription jobs.
   - Complete projects for various clients to build a diverse portfolio and gain exposure to several types of transcription work.

3. Obtain relevant certifications:
   - Research the most relevant certifications for your desired niche, such as Registered Healthcare Documentation Specialist (RHDS) or Certified Healthcare Documentation Specialist (CHDS) for medical transcription.
   - Complete the necessary coursework and exams to earn your certification, which will boost your credibility and employability.

4. Showcase your achievements:
   - Update your resume regularly with your latest transcription work, including details on the type of content you transcribed and the industries you have worked in.
   - Include any additional relevant skills, such as language proficiency or specialized knowledge, to make your resume more attractive to potential clients.

5. Network and expand your professional connections:
   - Join transcription and digital nomad communities on social media platforms and online forums to network with fellow transcriptionists and potential clients.
   - Attend industry events, workshops, and conferences to stay updated on the latest trends and establish new connections.

Build a professional online presence

A strong online presence is crucial for digital nomad transcriptionists looking to attract clients and grow their business. This guide will outline the steps to create an effective online presence that showcases your skills, services, and testimonials.

1. Create a professional website:
   - Design a clean, user-friendly website that highlights your transcription services, skills, and experience.
   - Include a portfolio section showcasing samples of your work, if possible.
   - Add a testimonials page featuring reviews from satisfied clients.
   - Make sure your contact information is easily accessible for potential clients to contact you.

2. Establish a presence on social media platforms:
   - Create professional profiles on LinkedIn, Facebook, and Instagram.
   - Share updates on your latest projects, industry news, and tips for effective transcription.
   - Engage with your audience by responding to comments, messages, and inquiries.
   - Join groups and communities related to transcription, freelancing, and digital nomad lifestyles to expand your network.

3. Join transcription communities and forums:
    *   Participate in online transcription communities and forums, such as Transcription Haven or Transcription Essentials.
    *   Contribute to discussions, ask questions, and share your expertise.
    *   Network with fellow transcriptionists and potential clients by offering advice and support.

4. Publish informative blog posts:
    *   Write and publish blog posts on your website covering topics related to transcription, such as best practices, industry trends, and tips for success.
    *   Share these posts on your social media platforms to increase visibility and demonstrate your expertise.

5. Optimize your online presence for search engines:
    *   Use relevant keywords related to transcription services in your website content and meta tags to improve search engine rankings.
    *   Create high-quality backlinks to your website by guest posting on reputable blogs or websites within the transcription industry.

Determine your niche and services

Specializing in a specific niche, such as medical transcription, can set you apart from the competition and lead to higher pay. This guide will outline the steps to develop your knowledge and expertise in your chosen niche, helping you to become a sought-after transcriptionist within that field.

1. Identify your niche:

    *   Assess your interests, background, and experience to determine which niche suits you best. Examples include medical, legal, technical, or business transcription.
    *   Consider the demand for transcription services within that niche and the potential for higher pay.

2. Develop industry-specific knowledge:

    *   Familiarize yourself with the terminology, jargon, and abbreviations commonly used in your chosen niche.
    *   Study industry-specific guidelines and formatting requirements to ensure your transcriptions meet the necessary standards.
    *   Learn about relevant laws and regulations that may impact transcription work in your chosen field.

3. Master niche-specific software and tools:

    *   Research and learn the transcription software and tools commonly used within your niche.
    *   Practice using the software to improve your proficiency and speed.
    *   Stay updated on new software releases and industry trends to ensure you are using the most current tools available.

4. Obtain relevant certifications:

- Pursue certifications that demonstrate your expertise and commitment to your niche. For example, consider obtaining the Registered Healthcare Documentation Specialist (RHDS) or Certified Healthcare Documentation Specialist (CHDS) for medical transcription.
- Add these certifications to your resume and online profiles to enhance your credibility.

5. Network with professionals in your niche:

- Join industry-specific forums, groups, and social media communities to connect with other transcriptionists, professionals, and potential clients within your niche.
- Attend conferences, workshops, and webinars to expand your network and stay informed about the latest developments in your chosen field.

6. Market your niche expertise:

- Highlight your niche specialization on your website, social media profiles, and marketing materials.
- Tailor your services to cater to the specific needs of clients within your niche.
- Offer free consultations or samples of your work to showcase your expertise and attract new clients.

Set your rates

Establishing competitive rates and finding clients are crucial aspects of running a successful business. This guide will help you determine your pricing structure and explore numerous ways to find clients and build your network.

1. Determine your pricing structure:

- Consider whether to charge per audio hour, per minute, or per word. Factors to consider include the complexity of the material, the quality of the audio, and turnaround time.
- Research industry standards and competitor rates to ensure your prices are competitive.
- Be prepared to negotiate with clients to reach a fair agreement, while still ensuring you are adequately compensated for your time and expertise.

2. Create a professional online presence:

- Develop a website that showcases your skills, services, portfolio, testimonials, and contact information.
- Establish a presence on professional social media platforms like LinkedIn and industry-specific platforms like Transcription Hub.
- Use your online presence to promote your niche expertise and differentiate yourself from the competition.

3. Find clients on freelance platforms:

- Register on freelance platforms like Upwork, Freelancer, or Fiverr to connect with potential clients.
- Create a compelling profile that highlights your skills, experience, and niche specialization.

- Be proactive in applying for relevant transcription projects on these platforms.

4. Utilize job boards and transcription-specific websites:

   - Browse job boards and transcription-specific websites, such as TranscribeMe or Rev, for freelance and remote transcription opportunities.
   - Tailor your application materials to highlight your relevant skills and experience.
   - Stay up to date with new job postings to increase your chances of securing work.

5. Network on social media and within transcription communities:

   - Engage with fellow transcriptionists and potential clients on social media platforms and within transcription communities.
   - Share valuable content, such as tips, insights, and industry news, to showcase your expertise and attract attention from potential clients.
   - Attend virtual events and webinars to expand your network and stay informed about the latest trends in the transcription industry.

6. Leverage word-of-mouth referrals:

   - Encourage satisfied clients to refer you to their network of contacts.
   - Request testimonials or reviews from clients, which can be showcased on your website and social media profiles.
   - Offer incentives, such as discounts on future services, to clients who refer new business to you.

Create a system for managing tasks and deadlines

As a digital nomad transcriptionist, staying organized is crucial for managing multiple projects, meeting deadlines, and maintaining a professional reputation. Utilizing project management tools like Trello or Asana can help you streamline your workflow and ensure you stay on top of your tasks. This guide will provide tips on using these tools effectively to manage your transcription business while working remotely.

1. Choose the right project management tool:

   - Assess your needs, preferences, and budget before selecting a project management tool.
   - Consider the features, user-friendliness, and mobile compatibility of Trello and Asana to determine which platform best suits your business requirements.

2. Set up your project management workspace:

   - Create separate boards or projects for each client or type of transcription work.
   - Use columns or lists to categorize tasks based on their status (e.g., pending, in progress, completed).
   - Customize your workspace with labels, tags, or colours to easily identify and prioritize tasks.

3. Break down tasks into smaller, manageable steps:

- Divide transcription projects into smaller tasks, such as downloading files, transcribing audio, proofreading, and delivering the final transcript.
- Create subtasks or checklists within each task to track your progress and ensure you do not miss any crucial steps.

4. Utilize due dates and reminders:

- Assign due dates to each task to ensure timely completion and delivery of projects.
- Set up reminders or notifications to alert you of upcoming deadlines and keep you on track.

5. Track client information and project details:

- Use the description or comments section of tasks to store essential client information and project details, such as file formats, special instructions, and billing information.
- Attach relevant documents, such as audio files, style guides, or invoices, directly to tasks for easy access and organization.

6. Keep communication centralized:

- Communicate with clients or team members through the project management tool to keep all correspondence in one place.
- Use the comments or messaging features to discuss project updates, questions, or feedback.

7. Regularly update and review your workspace:

- Update task statuses as you progress through projects and mark tasks as complete once they are finished.
- Periodically review your workspace to ensure tasks are up-to-date, deadlines are met, and nothing slips through the cracks.

8. Synchronise your project management tool with other productivity apps:

- Integrate your project management tool with other apps, such as Google Drive, Dropbox, or your preferred invoicing software, to streamline your workflow and maintain a centralized system.

Invest in quality equipment

Having the right tools is crucial for producing accurate, efficient, and high-quality work. Investing in quality headphones, a reliable computer, and transcription software can make all the difference in your success. This guide will outline the essential equipment and tips for choosing the best options to support your transcription business while working remotely.

1. Quality headphones:

   - Invest in comfortable, noise-cancelling headphones that provide clear audio and minimize background noise.
   - Choose headphones with an adjustable headband and cushioned ear cups for extended wear and comfort during long transcription sessions.
   - Consider wireless headphones for added convenience and mobility, especially if you frequently work in various locations.

2. Reliable computer:

   - Select a laptop or portable computer with sufficient processing power, memory, and storage to handle transcription software and large audio files.
   - Ensure your computer has a comfortable keyboard for extended typing sessions, as well as a high-quality display for reading transcripts and accessing software features.
   - Choose a computer with a long-lasting battery and lightweight design for easy transport and use while traveling.

3. Transcription software:

   - Research and invest in transcription software that offers features such as automatic timestamps, customizable keyboard shortcuts, and adjustable playback speed.
   - Look for software with a user-friendly interface and compatibility with your preferred operating system.
   - Consider using a cloud-based transcription software to access your work from any device and location.

4. Noise-cancelling headphones for noisy environments:

   - Invest in noise-cancelling headphones specifically designed to reduce ambient noise, making it easier to focus on audio files in busy or noisy environments.
   - Look for headphones with adjustable noise-cancellation levels to suit various situations, from crowded cafes to quiet home offices.
   - Ensure that the noise-cancelling headphones also have a quality microphone for any transcription work that requires audio input or communication.

5. Ergonomic accessories:

   - Consider investing in ergonomic accessories, such as a portable laptop stand, external keyboard, and mouse to create a comfortable and healthy workstation while working remotely.
   - Select accessories that are lightweight, compact, and easy to transport during your travels.

6. Reliable internet connection:

   - A stable and fast internet connection is crucial for downloading audio files, accessing cloud-based transcription software, and communicating with clients.
   - Invest in a portable Wi-Fi hotspot or choose a mobile data plan with sufficient coverage and data allowance to ensure you can work effectively from any location.

Continuously improve your skills

In the competitive transcription market, staying up to date with the latest trends, tools, and best practices is crucial for success. As a digital nomad transcriptionist, it is essential to regularly update and expand your skillset to remain competitive and provide the best service possible. This guide will offer tips on how to continually develop your transcription skills and knowledge, even while working remotely.

1. Online courses and tutorials:

   - Take advantage of online learning platforms, such as Coursera, Udemy, or LinkedIn Learning, to access transcription-related courses and tutorials.
   - Look for courses that cover topics like transcription techniques, industry-specific terminology, or specialized transcription software.

2. Webinars and virtual workshops:

   - Attend webinars and virtual workshops hosted by transcription experts, industry organizations, or transcription software providers.
   - Use these events to learn about new tools, techniques, and industry developments, as well as to ask questions and receive personalized feedback.

3. Networking and industry events:

   - Join online transcription communities, forums, or social media groups to connect with fellow transcriptionists and industry professionals.
   - Participate in virtual industry events, such as conferences or trade shows, to stay informed about the latest trends, tools, and best practices.

4. Certifications and training programs:

   - Pursue professional certifications or training programs in transcription, such as those offered by the American Association of Electronic Reporters and Transcribers (AAERT) or the National Court Reporters Association (NCRA).
   - These certifications can help enhance your credibility and marketability as a transcriptionist.

5. Expand your industry knowledge:

   - Familiarize yourself with industry-specific terminology and jargon by researching the industries you work in, such as legal, medical, or entertainment.
   - Stay informed about industry trends and developments by subscribing to industry newsletters, podcasts, or blogs.

6. Improve your typing speed and accuracy:

   - Regularly practice your typing skills using online tools like typingtest.com or 10fastfingers.com to increase your typing speed and accuracy.
   - Consider learning touch typing or shorthand techniques to further improve your efficiency.

7. Enhance language and grammar skills:

- Continually refine your language and grammar skills by taking online courses, reading books, or using language learning apps like Grammarly or Hemingway.
- Familiarize yourself with distinctive style guides and formatting standards used in transcription, such as the Chicago Manual of Style or the Associated Press Stylebook.

8. Learn new software and technologies:

- Stay updated on the latest transcription software, tools, and technologies by reading industry news, product reviews, and tutorials.
- Experiment with different software options and incorporate the most effective tools into your workflow to increase efficiency and productivity.

BUSINESS CONSULTANT

The digital nomad lifestyle offers the opportunity to travel the world while working remotely. As a business consultant, you can leverage your expertise to help companies assess their processes and maximize efficiency. A strong background in your chosen field is essential for success. This comprehensive guide will help you establish yourself as a successful digital nomad business consultant.

Assess your skills and interests

As a digital nomad, you may be looking to leverage your skills and expertise to become a successful business consultant. To excel in this career, you need to assess your skills and interests, ensuring they align with the requirements of the role. This guide will help you evaluate your abilities and give you insights into how to grow your business as a digital nomad business consultant.

1. Assess Your Skills and Interests - Before pursuing a career as a digital nomad business consultant, consider the following questions:

   - Do you have a strong background and expertise in a specific industry or field?
   - Are you skilled in analysing business processes and identifying areas for improvement?
   - Can you develop and implement effective strategies and solutions?
   - Are you comfortable working remotely and maintaining a reliable internet connection?

2. Identify Your Niche - To excel as a digital nomad business consultant, it is essential to identify your niche.

   - Start by examining your strengths and past experiences and choose a specific industry or field in which you have substantial knowledge. This specialization will make you more marketable and allow you to provide tailored solutions to your clients.
   - Develop Your Expertise - Join industry-related organizations, attend conferences, and participate in online forums to network and learn from other professionals in your field.

4. Build Your Portfolio - A strong portfolio is crucial in showcasing your skills and expertise to potential clients.

   - Create case studies of past projects that demonstrate your ability to analyse business processes, identify areas for improvement, and implement effective strategies.
   - Include testimonials from satisfied clients to build credibility and showcase your success.

5. Market Yourself - As a digital nomad, you need to have a strong online presence to attract clients.

   - Create a professional website that showcases your portfolio, highlights your niche, and details your services. Use social media platforms, blog posts, and guest articles to share your knowledge and establish yourself as an expert in your field.

6. Network and Build Relationships
   - Connect with potential clients and other professionals in your niche, both online and in person.
   - Attend industry events, join online communities, and participate in webinars to expand your network and establish valuable connections.

7. Maintain a Reliable Remote Work Setup
   - Invest in a high-quality laptop, secure and dependable internet connection, and communication tools like video conferencing software. This will ensure you can efficiently work from anywhere in the world and maintain open communication with clients.

- Do you have a strong background and expertise in a specific industry or field?
- Are you skilled in analysing business processes and identifying areas for improvement?
- Can you develop and implement effective strategies and solutions?
- Are you comfortable working remotely and maintaining a reliable internet connection?

Develop your skillset to be a successful business consultant

You will need a range of skills, including:

- Strong analytical and problem-solving abilities
- Excellent communication and presentation skills
- Project management and organizational skills
- Familiarity with relevant industry standards and best practices

Gain experience and certifications

Build your business consulting resume by gaining experience in your chosen field, either through employment or freelance work.

- Obtain relevant certifications, such as a Project Management Professional (PMP) or Certified Management Consultant (CMC), to enhance your credibility.

Build a professional online presence

A strong online presence is essential for attracting clients. Consider the following steps:

- Create a website showcasing your skills, services, portfolio, testimonials, and contact information.
- Establish a presence on professional social media platforms such as LinkedIn.
- Join industry-specific communities and forums to network with fellow consultants and potential clients.

Determine your niche and services

Specializing in a specific industry or offering a unique set of services can set you apart from the competition. Determine what type of clients you want to work with and what services you want to offer based on your skills and interests.

Establish competitive rates for your services

Based on your experience, expertise, and the industry standard. Consider whether to charge per hour, per project, or on a retainer basis, and be prepared to negotiate with clients to reach a fair agreement.

Find clients and build your network

There are several ways to find clients as a digital nomad business consultant, including:

- Freelance platforms like Upwork, Freelancer, or Fiverr
- Job boards and industry-specific websites
- Networking on professional social media and within industry communities
- Word-of-mouth referrals from satisfied clients

Create a system for managing tasks and deadlines

Staying organized is crucial for a business consultant. Use project management tools like Trello, Asana, or Basecamp to plan, schedule, and track projects. This will help ensure you stay on top of your work and deliver projects on time.

Maintain clear communication with clients

Clear and consistent communication is key to building strong relationships with your clients. Establish regular check-ins and provide status updates on your work. Be responsive to your clients' needs and be proactive in addressing any concerns or issues that may arise.

Continuously improve your skills

Stay competitive in the business consulting market by regularly updating and expanding your skillset. Take online courses, attend industry conferences, or participate in webinars to stay.

CAREER COACH

 The digital nomad lifestyle offers the opportunity to travel the world while working remotely. As a career coach, you can leverage your professional experience to help others succeed by guiding them through career planning, resume building, interview preparation, and more. This comprehensive guide will help you establish yourself as a successful digital nomad career coach.

Assess your skills and interests

To excel in your chosen field, especially as a consultant or freelancer, it is crucial to assess your background and expertise. This guide will help you determine if you possess the necessary knowledge and experience to succeed and provide valuable insights to clients.

1. Begin by examining your educational background and any relevant training or certifications. Consider the following:
   - Did you complete a degree, diploma, or other relevant education in your chosen field? • Have you participated in industry-specific training programs or workshops? • Do you possess relevant certifications or memberships in professional organizations?

2. Analyse Your Professional Experience.
   - How many years have you worked in your chosen field?
   - What types of roles have you held, and how have they contributed to your expertise?
   - Have you worked on diverse projects or with various clients, giving you a well-rounded perspective?

3. Evaluate Your Skills and Abilities.
   - Are you proficient in industry-specific software, tools, or methodologies?
   - Do you have strong problem-solving, analytical, and critical thinking skills?
   - Can you effectively communicate your ideas and findings to clients or colleagues?

4. Consult with peers, mentors, or former supervisors to gain insights into your expertise:
   - Ask for honest feedback on your strengths and areas for improvement.
   - Request an assessment of your skills compared to industry standards or benchmarks.
   - Discuss whether they believe your background and expertise are sufficient for your chosen field.

5. Investigate industry standards and compare your background and expertise to others in your field:
   - Research the qualifications and experience of other professionals in your chosen field.
   - Identify any gaps in your knowledge or experience that could put you at a disadvantage.
   - Look for ways to address these gaps, such as pursuing additional education, training, or certifications.

6. To maintain a strong background and expertise, commit to continuous learning:
   - Stay up to date with industry trends, news, and best practices.
   - Attend conferences, workshops, and webinars to expand your knowledge and network with other professionals.
   - Seek out opportunities for growth and development, such as taking on new projects or roles that challenge you.

Develop your skillset to be a successful career coach

Developing strong interpersonal and communication abilities is crucial for success in any field, particularly for consultants and freelancers. This guide will help you hone your active listening and empathy skills, enhance your knowledge of various industries and job market trends, and improve your resume writing and interview coaching expertise.

1. Enhance Your Interpersonal and Communication Abilities
   - Practice active listening: Focus on understanding the speaker's message, ask questions, and provide feedback.
   - Improve nonverbal communication: Maintain eye contact, use appropriate facial expressions, and maintain open body language.

- Develop effective written communication: Write clear, concise, and well-organized messages.

2. Cultivate Active Listening and Empathy
   - Remove distractions and give your full attention to the speaker.
   - Listen without interrupting and allow the speaker to finish their thoughts.
   - Validate the speaker's feelings and emotions by acknowledging their perspective.
   - Offer supportive and empathetic responses to the speaker's concerns.

3. Stay Informed of Industry and Job Market Trends
   - Regularly read industry publications, blogs, and news articles.
   - Attend webinars, conferences, and networking events related to your field.
   - Follow industry leaders on social media platforms and participate in online discussions.

4. Enhance Your Resume Writing Expertise
   - Study successful resume samples and templates from your industry.
   - Learn to use powerful action verbs and quantify achievements with numbers.
   - Tailor each resume to the specific job, emphasizing relevant skills and experience.
   - Proofread and edit your resume for grammar, punctuation, and formatting errors.

5. Develop Interview Coaching Skills
   - Familiarize yourself with common interview questions and effective response strategies.
   - Practice mock interviews with friends or family to hone your coaching techniques.
   - Teach candidates how to research companies and prepare insightful questions to ask during the interview.
   - Offer guidance on professional attire, body language, and other nonverbal cues.

Gain experience and certifications

As a career consultant or coach, obtaining certifications like the Certified Professional Career Coach (CPCC) or Board-Certified Coach (BCC) can significantly enhance your credibility and help you stand out from your competitors. This guide will provide you with an overview of these certifications and the steps to obtain them.

1. Certified Professional Career Coach (CPCC)
The CPCC certification, offered by the Professional Association of Resume Writers & Career Coaches (PARW/CC), demonstrates your expertise in career coaching and resume writing. To obtain the CPCC certification, follow these steps:

- Become a member of the PARW/CC: Visit the PARW/CC website and register as a member to gain access to certification programs, resources, and networking opportunities.
- Complete the CPCC training program: Enrol in the CPCC training program offered by PARW/CC, which covers essential career coaching topics, including resume writing, job search strategies, and interview coaching.
- Pass the CPCC exam: After completing the training program, take the CPCC exam, which consists of multiple-choice questions and a practical component requiring you to write a resume and cover letter.
- Maintain your certification: To keep your CPCC certification current, you will need to renew your membership with PARW/CC and complete continuing education requirements.

2. Board-Certified Coach (BCC)
The BCC certification, provided by the Center for Credentialing & Education (CCE), is a globally recognized credential that showcases your expertise in coaching across various niches, including career coaching. To obtain the BCC certification, follow these steps:

- Meet the eligibility requirements: Ensure you meet the eligibility criteria for BCC certification, including holding a minimum of a bachelor's degree and completing an approved coach-specific training program.
- Complete an approved coach-specific training program: Enrol in a CCE-approved training program that covers core coaching competencies, ethics, and professional standards.
- Accumulate coaching experience: You'll need to complete a minimum of 30 hours of coaching experience, with at least 70% of these hours being paid client coaching.
- Pass the BCC exam: Take the BCC exam, which consists of multiple-choice questions covering coaching theory, ethics, and professional practice.
- Maintain your certification: To keep your BCC certification active, you will need to complete continuing education requirements and renew your certification every five years.

Build a professional online presence

As a career consultant or coach, it is crucial to establish a strong online presence to showcase your skills, services, and expertise. This guide will help you create a professional website, leverage social media platforms, and network with fellow coaches and potential clients.

1. A well-designed website is essential for showcasing your services and expertise. Follow these steps to create an effective website:
   - Choose a domain name: Select a domain name that reflects your personal brand or your coaching business name. Register the domain through a reputable registrar like GoDaddy, Namecheap, or Google Domains.
   - Select a website builder: Choose a user-friendly website builder like WordPress, Wix, or Squarespace to design and create your website.
   - Design your website: Create a visually appealing and easy-to-navigate website that reflects your brand. Include the following pages:

     - Home: An introduction to your coaching services and a summary of your expertise.
     - Services: A detailed description of the coaching services you offer.
     - Testimonials: Positive reviews and testimonials from your clients.
     - About: Your professional background, expertise, and certifications.
     - Contact: A contact form or your email address and phone number for potential clients to get in touch.

2. LinkedIn is an essential platform for career consultants and coaches. Follow these steps to create a professional LinkedIn presence:
   - Optimize your profile: Ensure your LinkedIn profile is complete and up to date, highlighting your expertise, certifications, and accomplishments.
   - Share valuable content: Regularly share relevant articles, resources, and insights related to career coaching and job search trends.
   - Engage with your network: Like, comment, and share posts from your connections to stay visible and engaged in your network.

- Join LinkedIn groups: Participate in career coaching and industry-specific groups to connect with fellow coaches and potential clients.

3. Networking with fellow coaches and potential clients is vital for growing your business. Follow these steps to engage with career coaching communities and forums:
   - Research online communities: Find popular career coaching forums, Facebook groups, or Slack channels where professionals in your industry gather to share resources and advice.
   - Participate actively: Engage in discussions, share your insights, and provide value to the community by answering questions and offering support.
   - Build relationships: Connect with fellow coaches and potential clients by offering help, exchanging ideas, and sharing your expertise.

Determine your niche and services

As a career consultant or coach, specializing in a specific industry or offering a unique set of services can help you stand out from the competition. In this guide, you will learn how to determine your target clients and services based on your skills and interests.

1. Start by evaluating your own strengths, expertise, and passions. Consider the following questions:
   - Which industries or sectors do you have the most experience in?
   - What aspects of career coaching do you enjoy the most?
   - Are there specific demographics you prefer working with (e.g., recent graduates, mid-career professionals, or executives)?
   - What unique skills or experiences can you bring to your coaching practice?

2. Based on your assessment, determine the type of clients you want to work with. Some examples of target client groups include:
   - Professionals in a specific industry (e.g., healthcare, finance, or tech)
   - Individuals at a particular career stage (e.g., entry-level, mid-career, or executive)
   - Job seekers facing specific challenges (e.g., career changers, returning to the workforce, or individuals with employment gaps)

3. Define Your Unique Services. Once you have identified your target clients, develop a set of services tailored to their needs. These services could include:
   - Resume and cover letter writing for specific industries
   - Interview coaching for specialized roles
   - Personal branding for executives or entrepreneurs
   - Career transition support for career changers
   - Job search strategies for specific demographics (e.g., recent graduates, remote workers, or veterans)

4. To establish yourself as an expert in your niche, consider the following steps:
   - Obtain relevant certifications or training specific to your target clients or industry.
   - Attend industry conferences, webinars, or workshops to stay informed about the latest trends and best practices.
   - Network with professionals in your chosen industry to gain insights and build credibility.

5. Promote your specialized services through various marketing channels, including:
   - Your website: Highlight your niche services and expertise on your website's homepage and services page.
   - Social media: Share valuable content related to your niche on platforms like LinkedIn, Twitter, and Facebook.
   - Blogging: Author informative articles or case studies showcasing your expertise and the success of your clients in your chosen niche.
   - Networking: Attend industry events or join online communities where your target clients gather and showcase your expertise by participating in discussions and offering advice.

Set your rates

As a career consultant or coach, it is essential to set competitive rates for your services that reflect your experience, expertise, and industry standards. In this guide, you will learn how to establish your pricing structure, consider different charging methods, and negotiate with clients to reach a fair agreement.

1. Begin by researching the average rates for career consultants and coaches in your niche or target market. Factors to consider include:
   - Geographic location
   - Years of experience
   - Level of expertise
   - Certifications and qualifications

Use resources like industry reports, surveys, and competitor websites to gather this information and establish a baseline for your rates.

2. Take a comprehensive look at your own experience, expertise, and qualifications. Consider the following:
   - How many years of experience do you have in career consulting or coaching?
   - What certifications or specialized training have you completed?
   - How do your skills and expertise compare to others in your niche or target market?

Use this assessment to determine where your rates should fall in comparison to the industry standard.

3. There are several ways to charge clients for your services. Some common methods include:
   - Hourly rate: Charging clients based on the time spent providing services
   - Per session: Charging a fixed rate for each coaching session, regardless of the time spent
   - Package basis: Offering a bundle of services or sessions at a discounted rate

Consider which pricing structure best suits your business model, target clients, and the type of services you offer.

4. Create a Pricing Menu
Develop a clear and transparent pricing menu that outlines your rates for different services. This should include:

   - Individual service rates (e.g., resume writing, interview coaching, or career strategy sessions)

- Package deals (e.g., a complete career transition package or an executive coaching program)
- Discounts for returning clients, referrals, or group sessions

5. When discussing rates with potential clients, be prepared to negotiate. Keep the following tips in mind:
   - Be confident in the value of your services and the expertise you bring to the table
   - Be willing to offer discounts for long-term clients or larger projects
   - Be open to adjusting your rates based on a client's specific needs, budget, or circumstances
   - Always maintain a professional and respectful attitude during negotiations

Find clients and build your network

As a career consultant or coach, finding clients and networking effectively is crucial to growing your business. In this guide, we will explore how to leverage freelance platforms, job boards, social media, coaching communities, and word-of-mouth referrals to expand your client base and professional network.

1. Platforms like Upwork, Freelancer, and Fiverr can be excellent resources for finding potential clients. To make the most of these platforms:
   - Create a comprehensive and professional profile highlighting your experience, skills, and certifications
   - Develop a portfolio showcasing your past work and client success stories
   - Be proactive in bidding on relevant projects and responding to client inquiries
   - Maintain a high-quality rating and collect positive client reviews to boost your credibility

2. Many job boards and websites specifically cater to career consulting and coaching opportunities. Examples include:
   - The International Coach Federation (ICF) Job Board
   - The Muse
   - Coach Connector

Regularly browse these websites for potential clients and apply to relevant opportunities that align with your skills and expertise.

3. Network on Professional Social Media and Coaching Communities
   - Optimize your LinkedIn profile with a professional photo, compelling headline, and detailed work experience
   - Publish articles, share insights, and engage with relevant content to demonstrate your expertise
   - Join LinkedIn groups related to career coaching and participate in discussions to build your network
   - Connect with potential clients, industry professionals, and other career coaches to expand your reach

Additionally, join online coaching communities and forums where you can interact with fellow coaches, share best practices, and discover potential client leads.

4. Satisfied clients can be your best advocates, leading to valuable word-of-mouth referrals. To encourage referrals:

- Consistently deliver high-quality services and exceed client expectations
- Follow up with clients to check on their progress and offer additional support if needed
- Request testimonials and reviews from happy clients to showcase on your website and social media profiles
- Offer incentives or discounts for clients who refer new business your way

Create a system for managing tasks and deadlines

As a business consultant, staying organized is vital to ensure you effectively manage your clients, projects, and deliverables. Project management tools like Trello, Asana, and Basecamp can help you plan, schedule, and track sessions and client progress. In this guide, we will explore how to leverage these tools to enhance your organization and productivity.

1. Choose the Right Project Management Tool
   - Trello: Offers a visual, card-based interface, making it ideal for those who prefer a more visual approach to organization
   - Asana: Provides a comprehensive feature set, including task assignments, deadlines, and progress tracking, suitable for those who need a more detailed management system
   - Basecamp: Focuses on team collaboration and communication, making it an excellent choice for consultants working with a team or managing multiple stakeholders

2. Set Up Your Project Management Workspace

Once you have selected your tool, create a workspace to manage your consulting projects. This can include:
   - A separate board or project for each client, containing all relevant tasks, deadlines, and notes
   - Customizable labels or tags to categorize tasks by priority, status, or type
   - Task assignments to delegate responsibilities if you are working with a team

3. Use your project management tool to schedule client sessions, set deadlines, and establish milestones. This can help you stay on track and ensure you meet your clients' expectations. Consider:
   - Creating a shared calendar to schedule and manage sessions • Setting reminders for upcoming deadlines and milestones • Using recurring tasks for regular activities, such as weekly check-ins or monthly progress reports

4. Monitor Client Progress and Deliverables
   - Stay informed on each client's status and needs
   - Identify potential roadblocks or challenges early on
   - Ensure timely delivery of services and work products

5. Collaborate and Communicate with Clients and Team Members
   - Commenting on tasks for seamless communication
   - Sharing files and documents directly within the tool
   - Utilizing built-in messaging or chat features for real-time collaboration

Maintain clear communication with clients

Clear and consistent communication is vital for business consultants to build strong relationships with clients, ensure project success, and address concerns effectively. In this guide, we will discuss strategies for establishing regular check-ins, providing feedback, and being responsive to your clients' needs.

1. Set up a consistent schedule for client check-ins, tailored to each client's unique needs and preferences. This can include:
   - Weekly or biweekly calls or video conferences
   - Monthly progress reports or updates via email
   - Scheduled in-person meetings for local clients or when traveling

2. Offering valuable feedback on your clients' progress is essential to help them improve and achieve their goals. When providing feedback:
   - Be specific and clear about areas that require improvement
   - Offer actionable suggestions and practical solutions
   - Highlight successes and accomplishments to encourage continued growth

3. Demonstrate your commitment to client success by being responsive to their needs, questions, and concerns:
   - Respond promptly to emails, messages, and calls
   - Be available for unscheduled check-ins when necessary
   - Anticipate potential issues and address them proactively

4. Ensure clients feel comfortable reaching out to you by maintaining open lines of communication:
   - Share multiple contact methods, such as phone, email, and messaging platforms
   - Encourage clients to ask questions and express concerns
   - Be approachable and attentive during all interactions

5. Stay ahead of potential issues by proactively addressing concerns:
   - Regularly review project progress and identify potential roadblocks
   - Discuss potential challenges with clients and collaborate on solutions
   - Continuously monitor client satisfaction and adjust your approach as needed

6. Recognize that each client may have different communication preferences and adapt your style accordingly:
   - Adjust your communication style to match your client's personality and preferences
   - Be mindful of cultural differences and adjust your approach when working with clients from diverse backgrounds
   - Use different communication channels as appropriate, such as video calls, phone calls, or written communication

Continuously improve your skills

As a business consultant, staying competitive in the ever-evolving market requires constantly updating and expanding your skillset. By taking online courses, attending industry conferences, and participating in webinars, you can stay informed about the latest trends, tools, and best practices. This guide will provide strategies for continuous professional development to help you excel in your career as a business consultant.

1. Enrol in online courses related to your niche or to broaden your skills in other areas. Consider courses on:
   - Business strategy and management
   - Industry-specific topics
   - Emerging technologies and tools
   - Leadership and communication skills

2. Industry conferences offer opportunities to learn from experts, network with fellow professionals, and discover the latest trends and best practices. To maximize the benefits, be proactive in:
   - Identifying relevant conferences in your field
   - Planning your attendance to make the most of the available sessions
   - Participating in networking events to connect with potential clients or partners

3. Webinars provide a convenient way to stay updated on specific topics without leaving your home or office. To make the most of webinars:
   - Sign up for webinars hosted by industry experts and thought leaders
   - Engage in live Q&A sessions to deepen your understanding
   - Allocate time for reflection and application of the insights gained

4. Becoming a member of professional associations can help you access valuable resources and networking opportunities. Look for associations in your industry and consider the benefits of membership, such as:
   - Access to industry reports, research, and publications
   - Networking events and opportunities to connect with peers
   - Discounts on conferences, workshops, and other professional development events

5. Stay curious and committed to learning by engaging in self-directed learning, such as:
   - Reading industry blogs, books, and articles
   - Subscribing to newsletters and podcasts
   - Following thought leaders on social media

6. Earning additional certifications can enhance your credibility and demonstrate your commitment to staying current in your field. Research relevant certifications and consider the potential return on investment.
7. Collaborating with other professionals can help you expand your skills and knowledge. Consider partnering on projects, exchanging ideas, or even mentoring each other.

PERSONAL TRAINER

The digital nomad lifestyle offers the opportunity to travel the world while working remotely. For fitness enthusiasts, personal training is an excellent self-employed opportunity. By offering tailored services to specific clients, such as new mothers or individuals looking to build muscle, you can create a fulfilling and location-independent career. This comprehensive guide will help you establish yourself as a successful digital nomad personal trainer.

Assess your skills and interests

As a digital nomad personal trainer, you will have the opportunity to use your passion for fitness and health to help clients achieve their goals while traveling the world. Before embarking on this exciting career path, it is essential to assess your skills, background, and interests. This guide will help you evaluate your potential as a digital nomad personal trainer.

1. To become a successful digital nomad personal trainer, you should have a solid foundation in fitness and health. Reflect on your experience and consider the following:
   - Previous experience in fitness, such as working at a gym or as an instructor
   - Educational background in health, fitness, or a related field
   - Personal fitness journey and accomplishments

2. Designing and executing workout plans tailored to your clients' needs is a crucial aspect of personal training. To determine your proficiency in this area, consider:
   - Your ability to assess a client's fitness level and goals

- Knowledge of various exercises and workout techniques
- Experience in creating workout plans for different fitness levels and goals
- Adaptability in modifying workout plans based on client feedback and progress

3. Connecting with clients and helping them stay motivated is essential for a personal trainer. Reflect on your interpersonal skills:
    - Your ability to establish rapport with diverse individuals
    - Effectiveness in motivating clients to push their limits and stay committed
    - Communication skills, including active listening and providing constructive feedback
    - Problem-solving abilities to address client concerns or challenges

4. Consider Your Comfort with Remote Work and Technology:
    - Your experience with remote work or online training
    - Familiarity with video conferencing platforms like Zoom or Skype
    - Your ability to adapt to various work environments and schedules
    - Access to a stable internet connection and necessary equipment for online training sessions

Develop your skillset

As a digital nomad personal trainer, you will need a specific set of skills to succeed in this unique career. This guide will help you develop and hone your knowledge of exercise techniques and fitness principles, create customized workout programs, improve interpersonal and communication abilities, and gain a basic understanding of nutrition principles.

1. To become a successful digital nomad personal trainer, you must have a strong understanding of exercise techniques and fitness principles. Consider the following steps to strengthen your knowledge:
    - Obtain relevant certifications, such as NASM, ACE, or ISSA
    - Attend workshops, seminars, and conferences on fitness and exercise techniques
    - Learn from industry experts through podcasts, blogs, and YouTube channels
    - Consistently practice different exercise techniques to improve your skills

2. Creating personalized workout programs is crucial for meeting your clients' diverse needs. Here is how to develop this skill:
    - Understand your clients' goals, fitness levels, and limitations
    - Learn to design workout programs that incorporate various exercises targeting different muscle groups
    - Continually update your knowledge on the latest fitness trends and research
    - Obtain feedback from clients and adjust workout programs accordingly

3. Effective communication and strong interpersonal skills are essential for building rapport with clients. Take these steps to improve these abilities:
    - Practice active listening and empathize with clients' concerns
    - Develop clear and concise communication to explain exercises and provide feedback
    - Take courses or workshops on improving interpersonal skills
    - Learn to read body language and adapt your communication style accordingly

4. Nutrition plays a vital role in achieving fitness goals, and personal trainers should have a basic understanding of nutrition principles. To enhance your knowledge:

- Take courses on nutrition, such as those offered by NASM, Precision Nutrition, or ISSA
- Stay updated on the latest nutrition research and trends
- Learn to create meal plans that align with clients' fitness goals
- Understand the importance of macronutrients and micronutrients in overall health

Gain experience and certifications

As a digital nomad personal trainer, it is essential to create a solid resume to showcase your experience, skills, and qualifications. This guide will help you gain experience in the fitness industry, build a strong personal training resume, and obtain relevant certifications to enhance your credibility.

1. Before you can build a successful career as a personal trainer, you need hands-on experience. Follow these steps to gain experience in the fitness industry:
   - Apply for entry-level positions at gyms, fitness studios, or wellness centres
   - Offer your services as a freelance personal trainer or fitness instructor
   - Volunteer at local fitness events or organizations
   - Network with experienced fitness professionals and learn from their expertise

2. A well-crafted resume will help you stand out in the competitive fitness industry. Here is how to create an impressive personal training resume:
   - Highlight your experience, including employment, freelance work, and volunteer activities
   - List relevant certifications and training, such as CPR/AED and First Aid certifications
   - Showcase any specialties, such as weight loss, sports conditioning, or functional training
   - Include client testimonials or success stories to demonstrate your impact

3. Certifications can significantly enhance your credibility as a personal trainer. Consider obtaining the following certifications to boost your resume:
   - Certified Personal Trainer (CPT): Offered by organizations like the American Council on Exercise (ACE), National Academy of Sports Medicine (NASM), or the International Sports Sciences Association (ISSA), this certification demonstrates your competency in personal training.
   - National Strength and Conditioning Association (NSCA) Certification: This globally recognized certification focuses on strength and conditioning training, making it ideal for personal trainers specializing in athletic performance.
   - Other Specialized Certifications: Depending on your interests and target clientele, you may want to pursue additional certifications, such as:
     o Functional Movement Screen (FMS) for assessing movement patterns.
     o Corrective Exercise Specialist (CES) for addressing musculoskeletal imbalances.
     o Performance Enhancement Specialist (PES) for sports-specific training

Build a professional online presence

A strong online presence is essential for attracting clients and showcasing your expertise. This guide will help you create a website, establish a presence on social media platforms, and join fitness communities and forums to connect with fellow trainers and potential clients.

1. Your website serves as your digital portfolio, enabling potential clients to learn more about your skills, services, and experience. Follow these steps to create a professional and engaging website:

- Choose a domain name and hosting service
- Design your website with a user-friendly layout and professional images
- Highlight your skills, qualifications, and experience
- Showcase your services and pricing options
- Include client testimonials and success stories
- Provide contact information and an easy-to-use contact form

2. Establish a Presence on social media.
    - Instagram: Share high-quality photos and videos of your workouts, healthy recipes, and fitness tips. Use popular fitness hashtags to increase your visibility and engage with your followers through comments and direct messages.
    - Facebook: Create a business page to share your services, articles, and events. Join local fitness and personal training groups to engage with potential clients and establish yourself as an expert in your field.
    - LinkedIn: Build a professional profile showcasing your qualifications, experience, and recommendations. Connect with other fitness professionals, join industry groups, and share relevant content to position yourself as an industry leader.

3. Online communities and forums are excellent resources for networking with fellow trainers and potential clients. Consider the following steps to maximize your engagement:
    - Register on popular fitness forums such as Bodybuilding.com, MyFitnessPal, or Reddit's r/Fitness • Introduce yourself and share your expertise by answering questions and offering advice • Participate in discussions related to your areas of expertise and stay up to date on industry trends • Share your blog posts or articles to drive traffic to your website and showcase your knowledge

Determine your niche and services

Specializing in a specific niche can set you apart from the competition and attract your ideal clients. This guide will help you identify your niche, determine the types of clients you want to work with, and tailor your services to cater to their specific needs.

1. Start by reflecting on your own skills, interests, and passions within the fitness industry. Consider these questions:
    - What types of clients do you enjoy working with the most?
    - Are there specific fitness goals you are particularly skilled at helping clients achieve?
    - What unique experience or knowledge do you possess that could benefit a specific demographic?

2. Once you have identified your niche, conduct research to better understand your target market. This can help you tailor your services and messaging to better resonate with potential clients. Consider these steps:
    - Study the demographics, needs, and pain points of your target audience
    - Investigate the competition within your niche and identify gaps in the market
    - Keep up to date with industry trends and news relevant to your niche

3. Now that you have a clear understanding of your target market, you can tailor your services to cater to their specific needs. Here are some tips for refining your offerings:
    - Create customized workout plans and programs that address the unique challenges and goals of your niche

- Develop specialized packages and pricing options that cater to your target audience's preferences
- Offer complementary services, such as nutrition coaching or mindset training, which align with the needs of your niche

4. Finally, ensure your marketing strategy is designed to attract and engage your target audience. Follow these steps to make your messaging more relevant and appealing:
   - Update your website and social media profiles to reflect your specialization
   - Create and share content that speaks directly to the needs and interests of your target audience
   - Use testimonials and success stories from clients within your niche to build credibility and trust
   - Engage with online communities and groups where your target audience is likely to be active

Set your rates

Establishing competitive rates for your services is essential to attracting clients and ensuring your financial success. This guide will help you determine the best pricing structure for your business, considering your experience, expertise, and industry standards.

1. Begin by researching the going rates for personal trainers in the industry, considering factors such as geographical location, experience level, and specialization. Some resources to help you gather this information include:
   - Online personal trainer directories
   - Fitness industry reports and surveys
   - Competitor pricing analysis

2. Next, evaluate your own experience and expertise in comparison to other personal trainers. Consider factors such as:
   - Years of experience
   - Relevant certifications and qualifications
   - Client success stories and testimonials
   - Unique selling points (e.g., specialization or additional services)

3. There are several ways to structure your pricing as a personal trainer. Consider the following options:
   - Per hour: Charge clients based on the time spent working together. This is a straightforward method that makes it easy for clients to understand your pricing.
   - Per session: Charge clients based on individual sessions, regardless of their duration. This can be more flexible and may encourage clients to book longer sessions.
   - Package basis: Offer packages of multiple sessions at a discounted rate. This can help encourage long-term commitments and promote client retention.

4. Based on your research and self-assessment, determine your prices for each pricing structure option. Keep in mind that you may need to adjust your rates periodically to stay competitive and reflect changes in your experience or the market.

5. Some clients may want to negotiate your rates. While it is essential to value your services fairly, be prepared to discuss pricing options with clients and find a mutually agreeable solution. Consider offering:

- Discounts for new clients or long-term commitments
- Payment plans or instalment options
- Reduced rates for clients experiencing financial hardship

Find clients and build your network

Finding clients is a crucial aspect of your business's success. This guide outlines various strategies for connecting with potential clients, from freelance platforms to networking within fitness communities.

1. Utilize Freelance Platforms
   - Freelance platforms such as Upwork, Freelancer, and Fiverr offer opportunities for personal trainers to advertise their services and connect with potential clients. Create a detailed profile showcasing your expertise, certifications, and client testimonials to attract potential clients.

2. Social media platforms like Instagram, Facebook, and LinkedIn can be powerful tools for reaching a wide audience of potential clients. Consider the following strategies:
   - Create engaging content showcasing your fitness knowledge, client transformations, and workout tips.
   - Use targeted advertising to reach individuals interested in fitness and personal training.
   - Offer promotions or discounts to incentivize new clients to try your services.

3. Network within Fitness Communities
   - Building connections within fitness communities can lead to valuable word-of-mouth referrals.
   - Participate in online forums, attend fitness events and conferences, and join relevant social media groups.
   - Share your expertise and demonstrate your commitment to helping others achieve their fitness goals.

4. Obtain Word-of-Mouth Referrals
   - Existing clients can be an excellent source of new business. Encourage satisfied clients to recommend your services to their friends, family, and colleagues.
   - Consider offering referral incentives such as discounted sessions or free consultations to motivate clients to spread the word.

5. Partner with Local Gyms and Fitness Centres
   - As you travel to different destinations, reach out to local gyms and fitness centres to explore partnership opportunities.
   - Offer to lead group classes, provide personal training sessions to gym members, or collaborate on promotional events. This can help you tap into an existing customer base and expand your network in new locations.

Offer remote training services as a digital nomad personal trainer

Offering remote training services is essential to maintaining a flexible lifestyle while still providing clients with effective workout programs. This guide outlines the key elements of offering high-quality virtual training sessions.

1. Develop Online Workout Programs
   - Design customized workout programs tailored to your clients' needs, goals, and fitness levels.
   - Create detailed, easy-to-follow instructions for each exercise, including photos or video demonstrations to ensure proper form.
   - Provide variations and progressions to keep the program challenging and engaging over time.

2. Offer Video Consultations

   - Regular video consultations are essential for building rapport with clients, discussing their progress, and addressing any concerns or questions.
   - Use video conferencing tools such as Zoom, Skype, or Google Meet to conduct virtual consultations.
   - Ensure you have a quiet, well-lit space to conduct video calls, and invest in a high-quality microphone and camera for optimal communication.

3. Utilize Fitness Apps and Platforms
   - Leverage fitness apps and platforms to streamline client communication, monitor progress, and track workout data.
   - Apps like MyFitnessPal, Trainerize, and TrueCoach enable you to create personalized workout plans, set goals, and monitor client adherence.
   - Encourage clients to log their workouts, nutrition, and progress photos within the app, providing you with valuable insights into their progress.

4. Ensure a Reliable Internet Connection
   - A stable and fast internet connection is crucial for remote personal training services. Invest in a mobile hotspot or choose accommodations with reliable Wi-Fi to maintain seamless communication with clients.
   - Consider the time zone differences when scheduling consultations and be prepared to adjust your availability to accommodate clients in various locations.

5. Equip Yourself with Necessary Tools

   - To deliver high-quality virtual training sessions, invest in essential equipment such as resistance bands, a tripod for your camera, and any other portable fitness tools you may need for demonstrations.
   - Additionally, familiarize yourself with video editing tools to create professional-looking exercise demonstration videos and other fitness-related content.

Stay updated with industry trends

The personal training market is constantly evolving, and it is important for digital nomad personal trainers to stay up to date with the latest trends, tools, and best practices. This guide outlines several strategies to help you maintain a competitive edge in the fitness industry.

1. Take Online Courses
   - Continuing education is essential for staying current in the field of personal training. Enrol in online courses to learn new training techniques, nutrition strategies, and other relevant skills.

- Websites like Coursera, Udemy, and the American Council on Exercise (ACE) offer a variety of fitness-related courses for professional development.

2. Attend Industry Conferences
   - Participate in industry conferences, either in-person or virtually, to gain insights into the latest trends, research, and innovations in the fitness world.
   - Conferences like IDEA World, the National Strength, and Conditioning Association (NSCA) Conference, and the International Health, Racquet & Sportsclub Association (IHRSA) Convention are excellent networking opportunities and provide valuable learning experiences.

3. Participate in Webinars
   - Webinars are a convenient way to stay informed about new developments in the fitness industry. Many fitness organizations, certification bodies, and equipment manufacturers offer webinars on a range of topics, from exercise programming to marketing strategies. Sign up for webinars that align with your niche and interests to expand your knowledge and skills.

4. Stay Active on social media and Blogs
   - Follow industry leaders, fitness influencers, and fellow personal trainers on social media platforms like Instagram, Facebook, and LinkedIn.
   - Engage with their content to stay current on emerging trends and popular training methods. Subscribe to fitness blogs and newsletters to receive regular updates on new research, techniques, and tools.

5. Obtain Advanced Certifications
   - Pursue advanced certifications in specialized areas of fitness, such as corrective exercise, sports nutrition, or functional training. Obtaining specialized certifications not only enhances your credibility but also enables you to offer a broader range of services to your clients.

6. Network with Other Professionals
   - Connect with other personal trainers, fitness professionals, and industry experts to share knowledge, experiences, and best practices. Participate in online forums, Facebook groups, and LinkedIn communities to engage in discussions, ask questions, and offer advice.

GRAPHIC DESIGNER

The digital nomad lifestyle offers the opportunity to travel the world while working remotely. For creative individuals with knowledge of design software, working as a graphic designer can be an exciting and fulfilling career choice. By creating visual concepts for various clients, you can build a location-independent career. A strong portfolio is essential for success, and this comprehensive guide will help you establish yourself as a successful digital nomad graphic designer.

Assess your skills and interests

Before embarking on a career as a digital nomad graphic designer, it is essential to assess your skills, interests, and suitability for remote work. In this guide, we will help you determine whether you have the necessary expertise and characteristics to succeed as a digital nomad graphic designer.

1. Evaluate Your Design Skills and Expertise
   - Consider your proficiency in design software, such as Adobe Creative Suite, Sketch, or Figma.
   - Determine if you have experience creating visual concepts for various mediums, such as print, digital, and social media. Reflect on your knowledge of design principles, typography, and colour theory.

2. Analyse Your Industry Experience
   - Assess your experience working with different industries and clients.
   - If you have a diverse portfolio, this can increase your chances of finding remote work opportunities. Consider whether you need to expand your skillset or industry knowledge to improve your marketability as a graphic designer.

3. Assess Your Communication Skills
   - Effective communication is crucial for understanding clients' needs and delivering high-quality design work.
   - Reflect on your ability to communicate clearly and professionally through emails, video calls, and project management tools. Consider whether you need to improve your communication skills to enhance your remote work experience.

4. Evaluate Your Adaptability and Time Management
   - Working remotely as a digital nomad requires adaptability and strong time management skills.

- Assess your ability to manage multiple projects, meet deadlines, and adjust to different time zones. Consider if you need to refine your organizational skills to better manage your workload.

5. Consider Your Comfort Level with Remote Work
   - Evaluate your comfort level with remote work and maintaining a reliable internet connection. Assess your ability to find suitable workspaces while traveling, such as coworking spaces, cafes, or accommodations with strong Wi-Fi. Consider if you need to invest in portable equipment, like a laptop or drawing tablet, to work efficiently on the go.

Develop your skillset to be a successful graphic designer

Having a strong skill set is crucial for success in your remote work career. In this guide, we will outline the essential skills you need to excel as a digital nomad graphic designer and provide tips on how to develop and maintain them.

1. Proficiency in Design Software
   - Ensure that you have a strong understanding of design software, such as Adobe Creative Suite (Photoshop, Illustrator, InDesign), Sketch, or Figma.
   - To develop or maintain your proficiency, consider taking online courses, watching tutorials, or attending workshops to stay updated on the latest software features and techniques.

2. Understanding of Design Principles, Typography, and Colour Theory
   - A solid grasp of design principles, typography, and colour theory is essential for creating visually appealing and effective designs.
   - To strengthen your understanding, study design theory, read books, or attend design conferences.
   - Keep up with industry trends and best practices by following influential designers and design blogs.

3. Ability to Create Designs for Various Mediums
   - Being able to create designs for various mediums, such as print, digital, and social media, makes you more versatile and attractive to potential clients.
   - Practice designing for different formats and familiarize yourself with the requirements and best practices for each medium.
   - Keep your portfolio updated with examples of your work across various mediums.

4. Excellent Communication Skills
   - Effective communication skills are essential for collaborating with clients and understanding their design needs.
   - Practice active listening, clear written communication, and professional etiquette in all interactions.
   - Use video calls and project management tools to effectively collaborate with clients and team members.

5. Time Management Skills
   - As a digital nomad, time management is crucial for balancing work and travel. Develop strategies for managing multiple projects and deadlines, such as setting goals, prioritizing tasks, and using productivity tools like Trello or Asana.

- Be mindful of time zones and adjust your work schedule accordingly to ensure smooth communication with clients and team members.

Build a strong portfolio

Your portfolio is your most powerful tool for attracting clients and showcasing your skills. In this guide, we will discuss the steps to create a compelling portfolio that demonstrates your versatility and expertise as a designer.

1. Select Your Best Work
   - Carefully choose the design projects that best represent your skills, creativity, and versatility.
   - Aim to showcase a diverse range of work, including print, digital, and social media projects. This will demonstrate your ability to adapt to various design needs and appeal to a wider range of potential clients.

2. Create High-Quality Images
   - Ensure that your portfolio includes high-quality images of your work. Use professional photography or high-resolution screenshots to accurately represent the colours, textures, and details of your designs. If necessary, consider hiring a photographer or investing in a high-quality camera to capture your work.

3. Provide Detailed Descriptions
   - For each project, include a brief but informative description that explains the design process, client objectives, and any challenges you encountered and overcame. This will give potential clients insight into your problem-solving abilities and your approach to design projects.

4. Organize Your Portfolio
   - Organize your portfolio in a logical and visually appealing manner. Group similar projects together and use a consistent layout to create a seamless browsing experience.
   - Consider including categories or filters to help visitors easily navigate your portfolio and find relevant work.

5. Optimize for Online Viewing
   - Your online presence is crucial. Ensure that your portfolio website is responsive, easy to navigate, and optimized for both desktop and mobile devices.
   - Utilize search engine optimization (SEO) best practices to increase your portfolio's visibility in search results.

6. Update Regularly
   - Keep your portfolio fresh and up to date by constantly adding new projects and updating existing ones. This demonstrates your ongoing commitment to your craft and helps attract clients who are looking for the latest design trends and techniques.

7. Promote Your Portfolio
   - Share your portfolio on social media platforms, such as LinkedIn, Instagram, and Facebook, to increase visibility and attract potential clients.

- Participate in design communities, forums, and networking events to showcase your work and connect with others in the industry.

Gain experience and certifications

It is essential to have a strong resume that showcases your experience, skills, and certifications. In this guide, we will discuss how to build your graphic design resume to enhance your credibility and attract potential clients.

1. Gain Experience
   - Start by gaining experience in your chosen field, either through employment or freelance work.
   - Seek out projects that align with your interests and skills and diversify your experience by working on diverse types of design projects, such as branding, web design, or print materials.

2. Freelance Work
   - Freelance work offers flexibility and the opportunity to work with different clients and industries.
   - Look for freelance opportunities on platforms like Upwork, Freelancer, or Fiverr, and reach out to your network for potential projects.
   - As you build your reputation, you may receive referrals or repeat business from satisfied clients.

3. Internships and Entry-Level Positions
   - Consider internships or entry-level positions at design firms, agencies, or in-house design departments to gain valuable experience and build your network. These opportunities provide hands-on experience, mentorship, and exposure to a professional design environment.

4. Obtain Relevant Certifications
   - Earning industry-recognized certifications, such as the Adobe Certified Expert (ACE), will enhance your credibility and demonstrate your expertise in design software.
   - Other certifications, like the Graphic Design Certification from a reputable design school or online course platform, can also strengthen your resume.

5. Highlight Your Skills
   - Emphasize your design skills and software proficiencies on your resume, focusing on those most relevant to your target clients or projects. Be sure to mention your proficiency in Adobe Creative Suite (Photoshop, Illustrator, InDesign) and any other design tools or software you have experience with.

6. Showcase Your Achievements
   - Include any notable achievements on your resume, such as awards, design competition wins, or successful projects with significant impact. This demonstrates your commitment to excellence and helps differentiate you from other designers.

7. Include Testimonials and References
   - If possible, incorporate testimonials or references from satisfied clients or former employers. This adds credibility to your resume and gives potential clients insight into your work ethic and the quality of your designs.

Build a professional online presence

Having a strong online presence is crucial for digital nomad graphic designers to attract potential clients and showcase their work. In this guide, we will discuss the steps to build your online presence and effectively market your services.

1. Create a Professional Website - a well-designed website is essential for showcasing your skills, services, portfolio, testimonials, and contact information. Consider the following when creating your site:
   - Use a clean and modern design that reflects your style and is easy to navigate.
   - Include a homepage, portfolio, services, about, testimonials, and contact pages.
   - Ensure your website is mobile-responsive and loads quickly on various devices.
   - Use high-quality images and well-written content to make your site engaging and informative.

2. Leverage professional social media platforms to showcase your work and connect with potential clients:
   - LinkedIn: Create a comprehensive LinkedIn profile that highlights your experience, skills, and accomplishments. Share updates about your projects, industry insights, and design-related content.
   - Behance: Build a Behance profile to showcase your portfolio and gain exposure in the design community. Engage with other designers by commenting, appreciating, and sharing their work.

3. Join Graphic Design Communities and Forums
   - Online Communities: Join Facebook or LinkedIn groups dedicated to graphic design or digital nomad professionals. Engage in discussions, share your work, and offer helpful advice to others.
   - Forums: Participate in design forums like Reddit's r/graphic_design or the Graphic Design Forum. Contribute valuable content, ask for feedback on your work, and build relationships with other designers.

4. Share Your Work on Design Inspiration Websites
   - Submit your projects to design inspiration websites like Dribbble, Awwwards, or Designspiration to gain exposure and attract potential clients. These platforms can help you reach a wider audience and showcase your talent.

5. Write Blog Posts and Articles
   - Writing blog posts or articles about design topics can help you establish yourself as an expert in your field.
   - Share your insights, tips, and experiences on your website or as guest posts on reputable design blogs. This can also help improve your website's SEO, making it easier for potential clients to find you.

6. Collaborate with Other Professionals
   - Collaborate with other designers or professionals in related fields on joint projects, which can help broaden your network and expose your work to new audiences. This can lead to referrals and potential clients.

Determine your niche and services

Specializing in a specific niche or offering unique services can help you stand out from the competition. In this guide, we will discuss how to determine your niche and services based on your skills and interests.

1. Start by evaluating your strengths, weaknesses, and areas of interest. Consider the following questions:
   - What design skills are you most proficient in?
   - What industries or projects have you enjoyed working on in the past?
   - Are there any specific design styles or techniques you excel at?
   - What types of clients have you enjoyed working with?

2. Conduct market research to identify potential niches and services that align with your skills and interests:
   - Look for industries or markets with high demand for graphic design services.
   - Analyse the competition and identify potential gaps in the market.
   - Research trending design styles, techniques, or technologies that could offer new opportunities.

3. Based on your skills, interests, and market research, determine your target clients:
   - Consider demographics such as age, gender, location, and occupation.
   - Identify the types of businesses or industries your target clients belong to.
   - Determine their unique needs and challenges, and how your design services can address them.

4. Once you have a clear understanding of your niche and target clients, outline the specific services you will offer:
   - Create a list of design services that cater to your target clients' needs and align with your skillset.
   - Consider offering packages or bundles that combine multiple services for added value.
   - Clearly define the scope and deliverables for each service to manage client expectations.

5. Craft a unique value proposition that highlights your expertise, differentiates you from competitors, and resonates with your target clients:
   - Emphasize your specialized skills or industry knowledge.
   - Showcase your unique design style or approach.
   - Highlight any additional services or benefits you offer, such as fast turnaround times or unlimited revisions.

6. Ensure your portfolio and marketing materials reflect your chosen niche and services:
   - Update your portfolio with relevant projects that showcase your skills and expertise in your niche.
   - Tailor your website copy, social media profiles, and marketing materials to target your specific audience.
   - Include case studies, testimonials, or success stories that demonstrate the value you provide to clients in your niche.

Set your rates

Establishing competitive rates for your services is crucial for attracting clients and sustaining your business. In this guide, we will discuss how to determine the best pricing strategy based on your experience, expertise, and industry standards.

1. Start by researching the market and industry standards for graphic design services:
   - Study the rates of other designers in your niche or with similar levels of experience and expertise.
   - Research regional differences in pricing, as rates may vary depending on the location of your clients.
   - Look for industry reports or surveys that provide insights into average rates for graphic design services.

2. Consider your level of experience and expertise when setting your rates:
   - Higher rates may be justified if you have extensive experience or specialized skills in your niche.
   - If you are new to the industry, consider setting lower rates initially to attract clients and build your portfolio.

3. Choose a pricing strategy that best suits your services and workflow:
   - Per hour: Charge clients based on the time spent working on their project. This is suitable for projects with a flexible scope or when the time commitment is uncertain.
   - Per project: Charge a fixed fee for the entire project, regardless of the time spent. This is ideal for projects with a clear scope and defined deliverables.
   - Retainer basis: Charge clients a fixed monthly fee for a set number of hours or projects. This provides more predictable income and is suitable for long-term or ongoing client relationships.

4. When setting your rates, also consider the following factors:
   - The complexity and scope of the project
   - The estimated time and effort required.
   - The cost of any necessary resources, such as software or stock images
   - Any additional services or revisions you provide.

5. Clearly communicate your rates to clients and be prepared to negotiate:
   - Provide a detailed breakdown of your pricing, including any additional fees for revisions or extra services.
   - Be open to negotiation but set boundaries to ensure you are fairly compensated for your time and effort.
   - Be willing to offer discounts or incentives for referrals, repeat clients, or larger projects.

6. Periodically reassess your rates to ensure they remain competitive and reflect your growing skills and experience:
   - Review industry trends and competitor rates to stay informed about changes in the market.
   - Adjust your rates based on your increasing experience, expertise, or client demand.
   - Consider raising your rates as you develop a compelling reputation or specialize further in your niche.

Find clients and build your network

Finding clients is crucial for sustaining your business. In this guide, we will discuss various strategies to help you attract new clients and build a successful freelance career.

1. Leverage popular freelance platforms to find new clients:
   - Upwork: This platform connects freelancers with clients in need of assorted services, including graphic design. Create a detailed profile showcasing your skills and portfolio and bid on relevant projects.
   - Freelancer: Similar to Upwork, Freelancer allows you to bid on graphic design projects and connect with potential clients.
   - Fiverr: Offer your graphic design services as "gigs" on Fiverr, with set prices and packages. This platform is ideal for smaller or one-off projects.

2. Search for graphic design opportunities on job boards and industry-specific websites:
   - Regularly monitor general job boards such as Indeed and Glassdoor for graphic design positions that allow remote work.
   - Check design-focused job boards like Dribbble Jobs, Behance Joblist, and Authentic Jobs for freelance and remote opportunities.
   - Join industry-related websites and forums, such as AIGA Design Jobs and Smashing Jobs, to stay updated on the latest job postings.

3. Build your network and connect with potential clients through social media and design communities:
   - LinkedIn: Create a professional LinkedIn profile highlighting your skills, experience, and portfolio. Connect with potential clients and engage in relevant industry groups to increase your visibility.
   - Behance: Showcase your portfolio on Behance, a platform popular among designers and creative professionals. Engage with other designers and potential clients by following, liking, and commenting on their work.
   - Design communities: Join design-focused communities and forums such as Reddit's r/graphic_design or Designer Hangout to connect with fellow designers and potential clients. Participate in discussions, offer advice, and share your work to gain exposure.

4. Leverage the power of word-of-mouth referrals to attract new clients:
   - Encourage satisfied clients to recommend your services to their network.
   - Offer incentives, such as discounts or referral bonuses, to clients who refer new business.
   - Maintain strong relationships with your clients, as they may connect you with future opportunities.

5. Additional Strategies: Consider other methods to find clients and expand your network:
   - Attend industry events, conferences, and meetups to connect with potential clients in person.
   - Offer pro bono work or collaborate on projects with local non-profit organizations, which can lead to referrals and positive exposure.
   - Reach out to your personal network, as friends and family members may know someone in need of your services.

Create a system for managing tasks and deadlines

Staying organized is essential for managing your workload, meeting deadlines, and maintaining client satisfaction. In this guide, we will discuss how to effectively use project management tools like Trello, Asana, and Basecamp to stay organized and deliver projects on time.

1. Select a project management tool that best suits your needs and preferences:
   - Trello: Trello's visual, card-based interface is ideal for designers who prefer a visual approach to project management. Create boards for each project, add lists to represent various stages, and use cards to represent individual tasks.
   - Asana: Asana offers a more traditional project management experience, with task lists and due dates. It also provides various views, such as list, board, calendar, and timeline, to help you visualize your projects.
   - Basecamp: Basecamp is a comprehensive project management tool that combines to-do lists, file storage, and team communication. Its centralized platform is ideal for managing multiple projects and collaborating with clients or team members.

2. Set Up Your Projects and Tasks: Once you have chosen a project management tool, create a structure for organizing your projects and tasks:
   - Create separate projects or boards for each client or project to keep them organized.
   - Break down each project into smaller tasks and assign due dates to ensure timely completion.
   - Use labels or tags to categorize tasks by priority, type, or status.
   - Attach relevant files, such as design briefs, mock-ups, or feedback documents, to tasks for easy access.

3. Establish a Workflow: Develop a consistent workflow to manage your projects efficiently:
   - Organize tasks into logical stages or phases, such as research, ideation, design, revisions, and final delivery.
   - Move tasks through the stages as they progress, either by updating their status or moving them between lists or boards.
   - Regularly review and update your tasks to ensure they accurately reflect the current state of your projects.

4. Track Time and Deadlines: Effectively manage your time and deadlines using your project management tool:
   - Set due dates for tasks and milestones to ensure you stay on track.
   - Use calendar views or integrations to visualize deadlines and plan your workload.
   - Track time spent on tasks using built-in timers or third-party time-tracking tools, such as Toggl or Harvest.

5. Collaborate and Communicate: Use your project management tool to collaborate with clients or team members:
   - Invite clients or team members to join projects or boards, allowing them to view progress, provide feedback, and track deadlines.
   - Use built-in communication features, such as comments or messaging, to discuss tasks and share updates.
   - Keep communication centralized within the project management tool to maintain a clear record of feedback and decisions.

Maintain clear communication with clients

Clear and consistent communication is essential for building strong relationships with clients and ensuring project success. As a digital nomad graphic designer, you will need to establish regular check-ins, provide status updates, and address any concerns or issues that may arise. In this guide, we will discuss how to maintain clear communication with your clients while working remotely.

1. Establish Communication Channels and Expectations: At the beginning of each project, discuss communication preferences and expectations with your client:
   - Agree on the primary communication channels, such as email, messaging apps, or video calls.
   - Determine how often you will check-in or provide updates on the project.
   - Set expectations for response times and availability, considering time zone differences, and working hours.

2. Schedule Regular Check-ins: Regular check-ins are essential for keeping clients informed and engaged throughout the project:
   - Schedule weekly or bi-weekly calls or video conferences to discuss progress, address concerns, and gather feedback.
   - Send email updates or messages summarizing the work completed, any challenges encountered, and the next steps in the project.
   - Encourage clients to share their feedback and concerns during check-ins to ensure their needs are being met.

3. Use Visual Aids to Communicate Design Concepts: Visual aids can help clients better understand your design concepts and decisions:
   - Share mock-ups, wireframes, or sketches to give clients a clear picture of your ideas.
   - Use screen-sharing or presentation tools to walk clients through your designs during calls or video conferences.
   - Provide context and explanations for your design decisions, highlighting how they align with the project objectives and client requirements.

4. Be Proactive in Addressing Concerns or Issues: Anticipate and address potential concerns or issues before they become significant problems:
   - Regularly review project progress and identify any potential risks, delays, or challenges.
   - Communicate these concerns to the client as soon as possible, along with a proposed plan of action to address them.

   - Be open to feedback and suggestions from the client, working collaboratively to find the best solutions.

5. Be Responsive and Accessible: Maintain a responsive and accessible communication style to build trust with your clients:

   - Respond to client messages or inquiries promptly, even if it is just to acknowledge receipt and provide a timeframe for a more detailed response.
   - Be flexible in accommodating client requests for additional calls or meetings, within reason.
   - Keep clients informed of any changes to your availability, such as planned vacations or periods of limited internet access.

Continuously improve your skills

Staying competitive in the graphic design market requires continuous learning and skill development. As a digital nomad graphic designer, you will need to stay informed about the latest trends, tools, and best practices in the industry. In this guide, we will discuss how to update and expand your skillset through online courses, industry conferences, and webinars.

1. Online Courses and Tutorials: Expand your knowledge and skills through online courses and tutorials:
   - Explore platforms like Coursera, Udemy, Skillshare, or LinkedIn Learning to find graphic design courses that fit your needs and interests.
   - Look for courses on contemporary design software, techniques, or emerging trends in the industry.
   - Complete practical assignments and projects to apply your learning and build your portfolio.

2. Industry Conferences and Events: Attend industry conferences and events to network with fellow professionals and stay updated on the latest developments:
   - Research upcoming graphic design conferences and events, both in-person and virtual.
   - Choose events that focus on topics relevant to your niche or areas of interest.
   - Network with other attendees, participate in workshops, and engage with speakers to make the most of your experience.

3. Webinars and Virtual Workshops: Participate in webinars and virtual workshops to gain practical knowledge and insights:
   - Subscribe to newsletters or follow industry influencers to stay informed about upcoming webinars or workshops.
   - Attend live sessions or watch recordings to learn from experts in various areas of graphic design.
   - Engage in interactive sessions by asking questions, participating in discussions, and completing exercises.

4. Stay Informed on Industry Trends and News: Keep up to date with the latest trends and news in the graphic design industry:
   - Read industry blogs, magazines, and news sites to stay informed about new developments and trends.
   - Follow influential designers and design organizations on social media platforms.
   - Participate in online forums and communities to discuss industry news, share insights, and learn from other professionals.

5. Practice and Experiment: Regularly practice and experiment with innovative design techniques and software to expand your skillset:
   - Set aside time for personal projects that allow you to explore new techniques or software.
   - Challenge yourself with design prompts or competitions to push your creative boundaries.
   - Share your experimental projects on social media or your portfolio to showcase your versatility and growth.

WILLING WORKERS

Discover a Thrilling New Adventure as a Digital Nomad with World Wide Opportunities on Organic Farms (**WWOOF**).

WWOOF is a global network of national organizations connecting you to organic farm homestays across 210 countries. With no central list or organization, each WWOOF country organization upholds similar standards and works together to promote the values of WWOOF.

As a WWOOF volunteer, or "WWOOFer" (/ˈwʊfər/), you'll gain hands-on experience in organic and ecologically sound farming practices, contributing to the organic movement and immersing yourself in rural life or a different culture. While no monetary compensation is offered, hosts provide food, accommodation, and invaluable learning opportunities in exchange for your help in farming or gardening activities.

With stays ranging from days to years, you'll have the chance to tailor your WWOOF experience to your nomadic lifestyle. Your workdays will average around five to six hours, giving you ample time to connect with fellow WWOOFers from around the globe. WWOOF hosts include diverse farming environments, from private gardens and smallholdings to allotments and commercial farms. To become a WWOOF host, farms can register with their national organization or, in countries without a WWOOF organization, with WWOOF Independents.

Embrace the excitement of living and working on organic farms, while enjoying the digital nomad lifestyle. Join the WWOOF community and embark on an unforgettable adventure that combines sustainable living, cultural exchange, and personal growth. Your next life-changing experience is just a WWOOF away!

QUESTIONS

We would love to hear from you on what you found works / doesn't work / needs more information

/ needs an amendment or even a new addition (for which we will credit you).

contact@ConnectNomads.com

www.ingramcontent.com/pod-product-compliance
Lightning Source LLC
Chambersburg PA
CBHW060848220526
45466CB00003B/1282